The Northern Winter was coming on . . .

So we bought the town

Margaret Owen

A Los Angeles family's flight from the city into a jade treasure trove

MITCHELL PRESS / VANCOUVER, CANADA

Canadian Shared Cataloguing in Publication Data

Owen, Margaret
 So we bought the town

 ISBN Number 0-88836-020-7

 1. Frontier and pioneer life — British Columbia
 2. British Columbia — Description and travel — 1950-
*I. Title.
 FC3817.4.094   917.11′1   C77-002234-0
 FC1087.094

Printed in Canada
by
MITCHELL PRESS LIMITED
Vancouver

Dedicated to
the one whose restless spirit
made this adventure possible

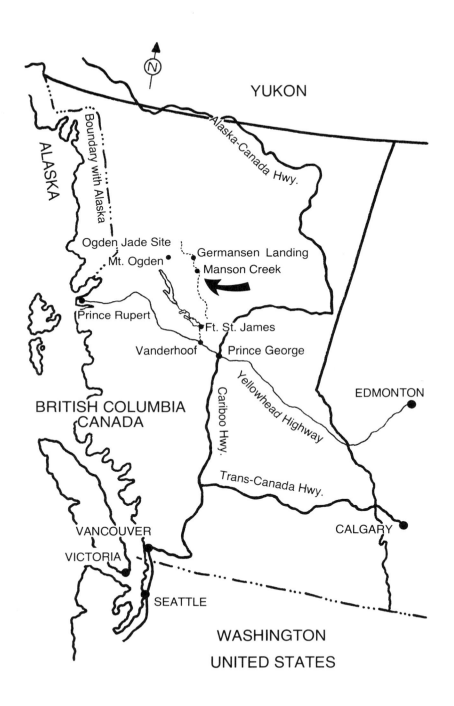

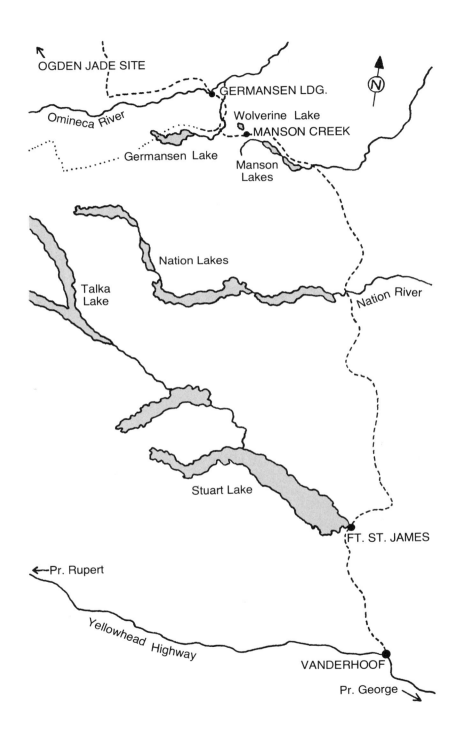

Contents

Publisher's Preface

The end of the story would be predictable.

There was the familiar speculation millions of Americans have engaged in: What would happen if they tore loose from the possessive city and just high-tailed it for the North Woods?

Left the crowds and the traffic jams, the pollutions of sounds and smells, the crime stories and the sameness of the supermarkets, the rising costs of land and housing, taxes and rents, the thrice damned eternal rat race.

Headed north with a congenial partner and his wife to share the experience and the much fewer but still inevitable odd problem of re-establishing in the wilderness.

Just go as far as there was a road to take you and when the light and telephone poles were left far behind and there was a solitude and a lake, stop and pitch your brand new tents. You'd have arrived — escaped.

You could build a log cabin against the snow and cold winds of winter and lay up a stone fireplace where roaring log fires would heat you. Then go on and build more of them until you had a hunting lodge set-up. Boy, that would be life, liberty and the pursuit of happiness — and happiness couldn't possibly evade your pursuit.

Never mind that you'd never hunted; that you knew somewhat less than nothing about how to build a log cabin; that you were not only in a foreign country but in an environment still more foreign than any foreign city would be.

So you were up in British Columbia's northern wilderness, your possessions ready to unload at an almost deserted ghost town, with winter — and the first realization of your changed life — coming on a-pace.

Any bush-wise Canadian or American could take it from there. He might deliver discouragement out loud but his face would certainly convey the message: Tenderfoot, turn around. You're city folk, you and your family and your friends.

There would be the harsh reality that it's harder and probably more costly to build a good log cabin than almost any other kind of house. That if you've never sighted a gun at big game, you'd better not aim at the hunting party trade. That wolf music on a still, dark winter's night can be noise pollution to ears accustomed to sociable city noises. And of course when the euphoria disintegrated under the batterings of minor and not-so-minor discomforts and duties of the genuine log cabin country, the impractical experiment in Dan'l Boone style livin' amongst the b'ars would come to an inglorious but welcome end.

The friends and neighbors who all knew it wouldn't really work out would be happy to invite such disconcerted adventurers back to where they should have stayed; and being good friends they would listen with varying degrees of polite interest to the losses of time and money the defeated had borne.

That should have been the end of the story of the Owens' contest with Nature in the raw. Nearly everyone would know that.

But we all like best the stories with a surprise ending. When Margaret Owen — more commonly Maggie — came to us with her story it surprised and pleased us enough to tell her to write it for all of us who would have known so well it couldn't possibly happen.

H. T. Mitchell
Publisher

Birth of an Idea

1

The deed has been transferred, money has changed hands, and now my young son and I are saying goodbye to the Canadian north woods which has been the only home he has known for ten of the twelve years of his life.

The grizzly bear invasions, the frightening accidental fires, the plane crash and incineration of the passengers, the thrill of finding one of the world's richest jade lodes, and other high points of excitement are no more to be remembered than are the recalled absolute silences of the woods, the crystal-blue skies which are not so clear even a hundred miles south, the beautiful newborn little moose which walked shakily and uncertainly around our yard after being temporarily lost from its mother, or the happy-sadness involved in the brief meeting of many wonderful people and then saying goodbye to them.

Today I am remembering. The long twilight has not yet turned to darkness and I have taken a respite from the packing job to relax on the porch swing. Inside the house all is confusion and disruption of normal living. Cartons and crates are piled high awaiting removal to another home in another part of the world.

But outside everything is unchanged. The cluster of cabins in the vicinity all stand silent with their streams of smoke from the stovepipes indicative of after-supper calm and contentment. The nearby mountain stands where it has always been, tree-covered and sheltering the creek for which the town is named. Without turning around to see it, I know every contour of Wolfridge Mountain behind the house, with little Slate Creek running at its base.

My thoughts are all nostalgic, recalling the advantages which our choice of this "bush" environment has had for our two live-wire daughters and infant son during their developing years. The girls were eleven and thirteen when we partly by chance and partly by plan made this big change in our way of living. The bright lights of Southern California were abandoned for gas lamps in this remote north woods area. The comfort and assurance of a steady income was traded for the hope of happiness in the wilderness. Living has been simple here, and income practically negligible in the beginning; but for a while we found it all — the good life, the "paycheque", and surprises and experiences beyond our imagining.

Not one of us could have known or would have guessed all this as we first travelled northward toward the tiny dot on the map which represented Manson Creek in central British Columbia. The enthusiasm and verve of the first week of the excursion had become a bit dust-covered as we bounced along over the final 120-mile stretch of graded dirt road, at a cautious pace of twenty-five miles an hour. We'd driven and camped for two weeks, and now here we were in the heart of the Canadian bush country, heading for an isolated spot two-thousand miles directly north of the densely populated Los Angeles area where we had spent our thus-far lives. I well remember my thoughts that day. Being a forty-year-old "city gal", accustomed to the normal creature-comforts of a middle-class suburban family, I wondered what was in store for all of us: a lot of unkown quantities, surely, but a few certainties in the form of outdoor toilet facilities, water by the bucket, few if any of the refinements we were all accustomed to, no schools, no stores. How were we all going to react to this primitiveness when it got right down to the basics of daily living?

During that long final drive to our destination, none of us could have foreseen or guessed that each of the family would settle in happily, grow and develop in his or her own way, influenced by and responding to the unusual environment. How could we have known that a major discovery of a mother-lode of jade was awaiting the methodical, persistent, encroaching footsteps of two men, one of them the man beside me? How could we then have guessed that Lyn and Les would find their future life-partners in such a remote spot? Least of all could I have foretold my own personal deep regrets when ten years later it would be time to leave what had become a rich, fulfilling way of life.

Remembering the earlier years of our marriage, I should have known that our future was destined to hold some important change from the ordinary way of life of the average family. Larry used to tell me of his boyhood dreams of someday sailing around the world, visiting exotic islands and port cities along the way. As a youngster he had studied maps and had planned many possible routes over the seas. Even before we were married he asked me how I'd like to take a world cruise someday in our own boat, perhaps even writing and illustrating a book of our adventures. Being more practically inclined, I classified him as the dreamer-type, but loved him enough that I figured it would be no problem taming him to normal civilized living.

And that's exactly what I did for many years, encouraging him through college after World War II, and then into a teaching position. His progression from school teacher to Assistant Principal and then to Principal of his own school was swift and natural because of his efficiency and effervescent personality. I could detect signs of restlessness, however, even while he was so effortlessly climbing the educational ladder. A prescribed way of life, year after year, was never going to satisfy this Larry Owen.

As a sideline interest during the first fifteen years of our marriage, we were buying, fixing up, and reselling several homes, a 38-foot yacht, and a mountain resort at beautiful Lake Arrowhead in the San Bernardino mountains. All of these projects were fairly successful financial ventures, but still something was missing for Larry. His restlessness sought release from a city existence.

Then, as though it had been arranged by the fates, we met a couple who likewise were ready for the adventure of something different. We were sitting around a log fire one cold winter night, lazily talking and dreaming aloud with some young friends, when Larry voiced a reflective thought.

"You know," he began, "this setting right now reminds me of something Mag and I have talked about before. Whenever my eyes get to burning from an unbearable smog-level, or when the freeway traffic piles up and slows to a crawl, my spirit yearns for freedom to breathe. I've desperately wished we could just chuck it all and take off to Canada or Alaska to try our luck at roughing it. A guy could do something like build a hunting-fishing lodge on a lake up there somewhere and have a wonderful life. How does that sound? We've considered this now and then, but hopes never germinate because we know we couldn't do it alone and we've never met anyone who shares enthusiasm for the idea."

It didn't take Robert long to respond. He straightened up perceptibly and his words came out in slow, measured precision: "By God! Wouldn't that be something! Wouldn't that just be the life!"

Carolyn, his wife, looked at him and then at us, wondering whether or not anyone was serious.

But Robert rambled on. "There'd be timber everywhere for building, and no shortage of wood to keep warm with. There's got to be large and small game and plenty of fish. No one would ever go hungry or cold."

There was a slight pause, and Carolyn, who had immediately fallen into the spirit of things, told us about pictures of hugely oversized vegetables she had seen and surprisingly they had been grown in Alaska.

3

Someone said, "Do you suppose one could build a greenhouse and grow vegetables up there every spring and summer?"

"If they can do it in Alaska, we could do it in Canada or wherever we wanted to," Robert boasted in premature, but positive assurance.

Larry looked at me and grinned. We both knew we didn't possess enough wilderness know-how to attempt a stunt like this alone, and right here with us now were the most likely candidates for partners we might possibly ever come in contact with again. Bob was the tall, lean, blond husband of the delightful, slim, blonde, Carolyn — both of them in their twenties. Larry and I were old enough to have been their very young parents; yet there seemed no generation gap in the warm friendship we shared with these young neighbors.

Just between you and me, I had always thought it a bit out of character whenever Larry talked about a hunting lodge. He didn't own a rifle, had never been on a hunting trip, and had no fever to kill animals. But still I'd supposed that one could perhaps own and operate a hunting lodge without going for the whole thing philosophically.

In practical skills and abilities, Robert would be a perfect complement in making such a venture successful. He was the hunting enthusiast of our fireside group, possessing an arsenal of rifles. Every year he would take off on an expedition with his dad or with a friend to bag a deer or an elk. By trade he was a construction man and on weekends was forever puttering over car motors or machinery. What a perfect combination of talents for the adventure under discussion! Carolyn, in her quiet way, appeared one who would willingly and happily follow her strapping young husband to the ends of the earth.

The spark of enthusiasm began to grow. One fantastic possibility led to another. We could start with two log cabins for our homes, make our own rustic — very rustic furniture, buy only what we had to buy, and as nearly as possible just live off the raw country. The following year we could build that lodge building and then advertise in Canadian and American outdoor-life magazines. It might be a lot of hard work in the beginning, but that wouldn't hurt any of us. Eventual success of such a project seemed assured. After all, what red-blooded hunter doesn't long to go farther and farther afield when the season is ripe for moose, caribou, deer, and other wild life?

Over the years past we had verbally romped through an adventure such as this with a few select friends; but on those occasions everyone, ourselves included, knew we were merely building conversational dream castles. From the first our discussion with these young friends was very different. We talked on and on into small hours that night and the visit broke up on a highly stimulated level. When we got together with Bob and Carolyn the next time I wasn't at all surprised to find that their enthusiasm had increased in the same ratio as our own. (I had a few personal reservations, but not enough to throw cold water on the ideas and hopes of everyone else.)

Robert's first comment when he next saw us was, "Well, how soon can we get started?" He and Carolyn were so enthusiastically eager that it wasn't long before we'd actually made the group decision to cut loose from Los Angeles and chance our futures on a dream.

It was a plan that should have ended in our becoming disillusioned and poorer but wiser, and deciding the city, after all, was a comfortable place to be and the old rut more habitable than the crude frontier, for city types like us. The Owen family stayed for the duration, adapted to the country and saw the adventure through to improbable success.

Pulling up Stakes

2

With no children, no home to sell, no difficult entanglements with parents, it was much easier for our young partners to come to a decision about up-rooting themselves from a routine nine-to-five life. Robert being a job-to-job construction man, it would be no problem at all for him to turn in his "notice". He and Carolyn could have been ready to start in a month's time. We, on the other hand, had two girls on the verge of teenage, a year-old baby son, a few pieces of property to sell or dispose of in some way, and Larry's school contract to finish. Although his parents always had bent backward to be unobtrusive in our family life, still Larry was their only offspring, our children their only grandchildren.

Since my mother had died a few years previously, and Dad lived alone, he depended on his married children for much of his social life. The prospect of our going so far away disturbed them all deeply, and I know that right up to the last moment they were desperately hoping that this drastic separation wasn't going to happen. My awareness of all our parents' feelings kept me in a bit of an inner turmoil, gravitating between the enthusiasm of my own family and the awareness of distress on the part of those we'd be leaving behind.

Our daughters were wild about the idea right from the start and kept the fire of enthusiasm fanned incessantly. Part of their excitement may have stemmed from the fact that in the northern wilderness — wherever that might turn out to be — they probably wouldn't be going to school anywhere except in our own log house. Unlike adults, who frequently see plans and hopes go awry, the girls had no negative thoughts concerning our proposed venture. It seemed advisable to extract promises from them to remain silent for a while just in case things shouldn't work out. They cooperated to a degree. Thirteen-year-old Lynlee told only a few of her very best friends. Leslee, our happy-go-lucky eleven-year-old daughter, probably forgot her promise the next day. At any rate, it wasn't long before we began hearing comments like, "What's this I hear about you folks going to Canada?" We'd shrug and answer that we might try it someday.

Since none of us had been farther north than San Francisco, we had no preconceived ideas of what to expect Canada to be like, except for what we'd seen in movies or magazines. To most people this northern country was surely best known for its spectacular Royal Canadian Mounted Police; and to this one bit of certainty we added a few guesses like maybe there'd be ten feet of snow, long frigid winters, log cabin housing, wild animals, Indians, and miles and miles of uninhabited land. None of us could remember spending much if any time in school studies on the subject of America's vast northern next-door neighbor. Although having made a career in the field of education, Larry suddenly realized that the school curricula with which he was familiar had shamefully neglected studies of Canada. This seemed strange since Canada is the second largest country in the world. We discovered, when we began questioning friends and acquaintances, that none of them knew much more than we. In fact, while talking to a waitress in a local restaurant, we mentioned that we would be leaving soon to try life in British Columbia. She expressed great interest and bubblingly asked if we had to cross the ocean! I was chagrined to think that even a small percentage of Americans could be that uninformed.

We set out to correct our personal ignorance by devouring everything available in reading material, and sent to the Canadian Consulate in San Francisco for any information that might be offered. We scoured the local library and watched advertisements in the *Los Angeles Times* for Canadian — especially British Columbia — property for sale. Whenever there was a good lead, out would come the map to localize the area. If it looked good, we'd send an inquiring letter asking for more details.

From the small wealth of information thus received, and from studying a large map of British Columbia, we concluded that our first choice for settling would be somewhere within a large area we circled in the central part of the province. This area was extravagantly endowed with lakes, and included only a few small settlements. Just one road headed directly north into this area from the east-west highway which bisected the province at its mid-latitude. There were big areas of unpopulated, virgin country in the upper two-thirds of Canada's map. We came to the conclusion we'd never be crowded in any area we might choose, and there was no hurry about making the choice. So what was wrong with taking off and just driving north until we found what seemed right?

We're off!

While the year of Larry's school contract was working itself out and the "For Sale" signs on our properties awaited responsive developments, the time was put to good advantage in very practical ways. Robert and Larry thoroughly investigated which types of vehicles would best make the trip and also be most useful after arriving at our destination. They studied lists of U.S. Army mothballed equipment which had been put up for auction, and took trips out to the desert town of Barstow to look over the field of trucks before making a bid. After all that, they spotted a truck which was parked in a yard only a few blocks from Robert's home, advertising itself for sale with a sign in the windshield. It was a heavy-duty Dodge army weapons-carrier, in excellent condition, eager to travel, and required only five-hundred dollars cash to buy. That was the first acquisition.

Next they decided the truck should pull a trailer, so back they went to Barstow and picked up a two-wheel, heavy-duty piece of equipment. After a few minor repairs, a paint job, the replacement of a few of the huge, worn 900 x 16 work-horse tires, the building of ribs for canopy tops over both truck and trailer, and the designing and applying of the canvas covers for same, we stood back to admire a good-looking and utilitarian half of our caravan. The other half turned out to be a Jeep station-wagon which we purchased from a friend. This Jeep would carry our family comfortably and would pull Robert's fifteen-foot outboard boat and trailer.

As time went on the lists began to accumulate: lists of things to buy (warm clothing for everyone, building and repairing tools of all types, camping equipment, sleeping bags); lists of things to sell (the furniture we wouldn't want, and a car); things to pack and store (dishes and silverware, treasures of possessions and clothing not needed but too valuable to part with); food to stock up on that we might be unable to buy in Canada; and on and on went the lists.

Carolyn and I kept our eyes and ears open for wildlife food recipes, all the latest in dehydrated foods, and absolutely anything which could conceivably apply to wilderness living and thereby make things a bit more fun and comfortable.

Preliminary preparations wisely included a trip to the dentist for each member of the group. All teeth were examined and repaired where required. A series of shots and vaccinations at the medical office was next. Our doctor was interested and helpful when we told him of our plans. He put together a most adequate medical kit and instructions for its use. Perfect for our needs was an only slightly out-dated medical book which he also included.

Time passed and things were getting accomplished. Most of our friends thought we were balmy, and acquaintances expressed a polite, eager interest in just what we were going to do and where we were going. Relatives had given up trying to dissuade us. We tried to relieve the minds of our loved ones by saying that we'd probably tire of adventuring in a couple of years and be back to take up where we had left off. Actually, I thought we would. Wishful thinking on my part, perhaps. I still wasn't totally in favor of the trip.

Finally, about fifteen months after that night around the fire when the idea was brought out of incubation, the day of departure had arrived. It was July 1st of 1963. We tried to hold our enthusiasm in check since most of the relatives were sad and tearful. Robert's parents were helpful and wished us well right up to the moment of leaving. Carolyn's folks were in Arkansas so they were uninvolved except by mail. Although my father was stoic, I saw tears coursing down his eighty-year-old cheeks. I had the distinct feeling that I would not see him again. Larry's folks were desolate and were convinced they'd never see us again.

After the last hugs and tears and goodbyes we jumped into the trucks and started the caravan a-rolling. What a sight we must have been! In the lead were Bob and Carolyn in the big army truck and trailer which were packed with belongings to the almost bursting ribs, and looking for all the world like a motorized covered wagon train. Right behind them was our family in the jeep which was pulling the boat. Since we had decided to camp all the way, the tents, sleeping bags and all camping equipment had been stashed in the boat for easy availability. Food and cooking gear to be used en route were packed conveniently at the back of the truck. This was a well organized adventure.

It was hard to believe we were actually on our way. We got all of eighteen miles from home and were ascending the nearby mountain pass when our first truck trouble developed. The problem was minor, however, and we were soon off again, laughing.

Our spirits were so high that at midnight, just for a lark, we stopped at a little roadside restaurant for coffee and cocoa and doughnuts. No one was sleepy, but by 2:00 a.m. we realized we'd be exhausted the next day and there were many, many miles to go, so we pulled into a mountain campground, extracted sleeping bags and slept soundly until well into the next morning.

It took three days of casual driving to go north through California. Each evening we slept out under the stars in our new sleeping bags. Meals were cooked on two Coleman stoves. We would stop to shop for current food needs about every second or third day. A minimum of restaurant eating was done. We had decided to have as much fun and at the same time be as frugal as possible until we reached our destination and knew what we were facing. Each day we mailed post cards to our folks back home so they could watch our progress and knew we were thinking of them.

The state of Oregon was crossed leisurely in one day and although there had been minor irritations with the trucks, no real problems developed until we were well into Washington on the fifth day out. The Jeep suddenly started pouring out vast quantities of blue smoke from the exhaust. We pulled over to the side of the highway so Bob could have a look. The diagnosis: a blown gasket. Calamity! While Larry drove back to the last town to buy a new gasket, Bob went to work under the hood, and the rest of us were confined inside because of the 70 mph traffic whizzing by and rocking the truck with each passing.

It was five hours before the motor was ready to be turned on again — and still it wasn't right. We were desolate. What should we do? There was talk of trading in the old heap for a newer model, but that wasn't serious talk. For the time being we hired a tow-truck to haul us back the few miles to Yakima State Park where we could relax and assess the situation calmly. What a spectacle we were, winding our way through the curving roads of the lovely park with the tow-truck hauling the jeep and accompanying boat, and the canopy-topped army truck and trailer bringing up the rear.

On closer investigation Robert discovered the problem to be a shot piston, and the job of replacement took the best part of two days, doing it the hard way without benefit of proper equipment and a garage to work in. But with determination almost anything can be accomplished even in trying circumstances. Robert was a good mechanic.

Carolyn and I took full advantage of the time. Already we'd been five days on the road and the pile of dirty clothes had mounted up, plus seven bodies in need of bathing. After the July Fourth holiday week-end picnickers had departed and with the park to ourselves, Carolyn and I went to work. We hand-washed the clothes and draped them over bushes to dry. Then we all used the facilities of the washrooms to take sponge baths, all the time feeling guilty knowing that the powers-that-be would frown if they knew what was going on. We always made it a point, however, to leave a place as tidy as we had found it, if not more so. The rear ends of the truck and Jeep had become rather cluttered so we rearranged everything and with all that housekeeping accomplished we felt as lively as on the first day of the trip. With the truck in good running order and Canada beckoning, off we went again.

The border was not far away now and we had done some thinking and speculating on the possibility and practicality of going on through Canada to Alaska. Why not! We had made the break, we were now completely on our own, and we might never have a better chance to see the forty-ninth state. There was just one drawback to consider carefully. It was now July, and summer in the north country was well on its way. If we were going to build cabins by a lake somewhere, we should be getting started without delay. September would be the latest we could still house ourselves in tents and be comfortable. The Alaska decision was left dangling as we continued north.

Into the Canadian North   4

A week after leaving home we reached the Canadian border immigration and customs station at Osoyoos. Crossing national boundaries was a new experience to all of us, and this one turned out to be so simple and uneventful that I think we were a little disappointed. There were no pages of forms to fill out, no big unloading of goods, no inspections, no hassle of any kind. We merely answered a few questions, mentioned that we might go on through to Alaska, were given thirty-day permits and were waved on. That continent-wide "undefended border" of oratorical fame did, indeed, bespeak friendship.

Leaving our homeland behind we began the next lap of the trip — heading up into the heart of Canada's Pacific province. It seemed an unprecedented experience to look at the map and see only this one highway connecting the southern and northern extremities of British Columbia, since back in California intricate networks of paved roads led into every nook and corner of the state. Things were different already.

We had at least five-hundred miles of travel on this major artery facing us, and it proved to be unusual in many ways. The miles through the spectacular upper Fraser River route were thrilling; the small towns and farms along the way delightful. We didn't pass through a single city remotely reminiscent in terms of size to Los Angeles or any of its suburbs, and that was the happiest part of all. We felt that we'd left all the rush and frantic pace behind.

But at Prince George, halfway up the province, a major decision faced us. This was the only crossroads point in our entire trip: should we continue north toward Alaska, or veer west to Vanderhoof and then north into the bush country? We felt that a matter of this magnitude should be pondered at leisure in comfortable surroundings, so we rented motel rooms for the night. After baths, changes of clothes, and sumptuous restaurant fare, we were ready to face the matter head-on.

As it turned out it was no big decision at all. No one had any strong feelings about getting to Alaska, so the deciding factor in staying with the original idea was the lateness of the year.

Next morning, after a good night's sleep, we directed our course to Vanderhoof, sixty miles west on the Yellowhead Highway. It's from this small town that the road takes off north into the bush and extends almost two hundred miles. Since Vanderhoof would be the last town of any size we'd be passing through, we wisely decided to check with a realtor there to find out how one goes about buying land in Canada.

Only Larry and I went in at first, introduced ourselves, and Larry confidently stated, "We've come from California and are interested in buying a piece of land by a lake somewhere up here. We have no idea how this is accomplished. Will you tell us?"

"Well, folks, I hate to disappoint you," the man began, "but lake property is just *not for sale*. The government has all lake frontage tied up. Now let's start at the beginning and see if there's some way we can help you."

Astonished and stunned, we went to the door and called our partners to come in to hear this devastating news. While the salesman tried to be of help, and directed our attention to ranches, acreages, large homes in the country, businesses for sale. Nothing seemed right. We were crushed.

"Gloria, could you come over here a moment?" our salesman called across the office. As he turned us over to a very charming and efficient woman, he said, "Folks, this is Mrs. Hobson, and she knows this part of the country better than any of us here."

So we briefed Mrs. Hobson on what we had been interested in and explained that now we were thoroughly perplexed as to which way to turn. She was listening as she riffled through sheets and notes on various listings.

"Here's something you might like," she ventured. "It's forty miles west of Vanderhoof on the highway, but it's definitely rural — four-hundred acres of arable ground which includes three-hundred feet of frontage which is at least lake-view. The price is ninety-five hundred dollars."

Only $9500 for 400 acres! We couldn't believe it! After dealing in a fair number of real estate transactions in California and seeing a forty-foot lake-front lot sell for thirty-five thousand, this was unbelievable. We had to see it. Mrs. Hobson told us just how to get there, and that there was an old deserted house on the property in which we could camp for the night. She would come out the next day to walk the lines with us.

We had no trouble finding the place and spent the afternoon and evening looking around. There was lots of ground, no nearby neighbors, possibilities unlimited for cattle, crops, and a small farm, but nothing seemed to strike just the right note. When Mrs. Hobson came out the next day we had already decided that this wasn't what we wanted. The price was unbelievably low and it would probably be a tremendous investment, but it just wasn't for us.

So back to the Vanderhood office we all went, hoping that she could come up with another idea. We were feeling quite congenial with these people by now, and one of the salesmen revealed to us that Gloria's husband, "Rich" Hobson, was the author of three successful books dealing with his ranching experiences a few decades earlier in central British Columbia. There was community pride evidenced when the salesman said that Hollywood had approached the Hobsons about the possibilities of making a film of one of the books. We were amazed, quite thrilled, and thoroughly awed. Hollywood and all it represented seemed so far removed from the simple, unhurried life in Vanderhoof.

Mrs. Hobson broke in. "Here's something up north, but you wouldn't be interested in this — I don't think so." Without looking up she went on persuing the listings.

"What do you have there?" Larry asked. "We had planned on going farther north anyway."

"It's a little settlement called Manson Creek, with a store, post office, a house and a few rental cabins. It wouldn't do for a family, though. The road is closed all winter. There are no schools for the children, no doctors, not even a radio-phone. There used to be one in the old Hudson Bay house before it burned down a few years ago. And mail comes in by plane only once a month."

We all looked at one another, visibly warming to the prospect, and Robert asked, "What's the price of this place?"

"Seventy-five hundred, plus cost of the stock in the store," she replied.

We couldn't believe it! Twice now in as many days we had been amazed by the vast difference between property values here and back home. Larry spoke first, so enthusiastically that who could refuse? "Let's go see it. We've got to see it!"

Mrs. Hobson shook her head in dismay but said she'd give us a letter of introduction to the owners of the place. Thus armed, we began the arduous 160-mile trip northward, heading into the very same area we had circled on the map twenty months earlier.

First Impressions 5

There are paved roads and there are dirt roads, and occasionally the twain do meet. We left the pavement at Vanderhoof and began the long stretch of dirt road indicated on the map by a dotted line which, interpreted, means "unimproved". And that's exactly what it was. Evidently improvements were in progress because "Sorry for the Inconvenience" signs had been posted by the Department of Highways, and periodically we'd meet men and equipment at work. But this was the very early stages of the improving and the clouds of dust stirred up by the occasional passing vehicle made vision and progress impossible for a few minutes until the dust settled.

Two hours and forty miles later we pulled into the first and only town along the way. Fort St. James is a quaint little place — a small logging town located at the lower end of beautiful Stuart Lake. It was one of the earliest Hudson's Bay Company outposts in the province, and was actually the first capital of British Columbia when the area, in days of earliest exploration and fur-trade colonization, was called New Caledonia.

The main road winding through town in broad curves was bordered by gas stations, churches, a post office, small stores, and a sprinkling of residences — of both frame and log construction. Visible in the background were patches of Indian Reserve housing, logging operations, huge beehive sawdust burners belching blue-white smoke, one small tract of newer houses, a school, and surprisingly, a beautiful modern two-storey hotel located at the lake shore. Nestled in one of the bays was a float-plane base with accompanying docks and a couple of planes idly bobbing at anchor.

After looking around town and indulging in snacks at a little corner restaurant, we climbed back into the vehicles and pushed on, knowing full well that a long, long 120 miles on this "dotted line" still faced us.

The dirt road didn't seem to get any worse the farther north we went, and only a very few cars passed us, so most of the dust we raised whirled around behind us. The scenery was miles and miles of trees and bush with innumerable little streams and creeks, bridges, and occasional lakes visible through the trees. Sometimes the road would climb to a summit and dip again, continuing on in its sameness. About the time lethargy began to settle in, the Nation River bridge came into view. We found out later that this is the area of the Continental Divide, which means that in this region the Nation River is the first of the northern waterways to flow north to the Arctic Ocean; south of this point all rivers take a south-westerly route to the Pacific. We were high enough north to be crossing the continental divide, but in what appeared to be no sharp roof-like peak.

We stopped on the bridge for a leg-stretch and a snack, since we'd done about sixty miles of non-stop driving, probably averaging twenty-five miles an hour. The view from the bridge is dramatic. Looking upstream, the river flowed toward us through a gorge, temporarily a prisoner between two cliffs. But on the downstream side we saw a panorama of meadow and a fanned-out, smooth and quiet-running wide river. This rugged, beautiful spot appealed to us all, and we filed away for future consideration the possibility of establishing some sort of commercial rest stop right here, since this appeared to be almost the exact halfway point between Manson and "the Fort". I liked it for another reason. It seemed to me that we'd gone far enough into isolation already. I had happily agreed that it would be fun to live near a lake up north, but we'd already passed lots of lakes in Canada. Our intended destination was a little town with a very small business enterprise, but it was difficult to visualize anyone driving this far over a dirt road for the pleasure of a holiday in the wilds. Our ten days of unsettled living out of the back of trucks, meals in the open, only an occasional motel stop for bathing, and the thinking and doing for our two young girls and the baby — all this was beginning to have an effect on this "city gal". I didn't voice my thoughts, but my personal consolation at this point was that surely things could only get better.

Back in the vehicles and continuing on again, I felt confident we were on the last leg of this adventurous trip. The real estate woman had said there were cabins and a house at Manson. That sounded good to me. I'd urge buying the place if only to have a spot to unload and settle down for a while.

My thoughts as, temporarily uprooted from city routines, we drove on and on concerned Larry's and my restless life up to this point. We had lived in our Los Angeles home for three years, but decided to move thirty miles closer to Larry's work when he got his first teaching job in the

Norwalk-LaMirada district. The next home was located in a brand new housing development in Downey. We lived there happily for eight years, became quite community involved, and the roots were down and taking hold when suddenly the urge for a change in environment became the most important thing in Larry's life. We made the switch to a more luxurious home in Orange County, thirty miles removed, in the other direction, from his school; but he could make his daily trip on the freeway in about a half-hour each way. After only a couple more years my questing husband longed to get on with the accomplishing of his dream of sailing around the world. Half fearfully and half enthusiastically the girls and I learned to become yachtsmen along with him on the 38-foot ketch we were able to acquire by swapping for it the equity in our home. Four months of family-living on the yacht and sailing around between Catalina Island and the Newport Yacht Harbor brought Larry's thinking back to more practical terms, and we let it be known that the good ship *Freya* was for sale.

The next venture was the mountain lodge. Things became lively again, with our life-style once more very much people-involved. We were constantly meeting new friends. It was busy and hectic, and especially so after the birth of our infant son, Everett. Thinking back, it's hard to remember or even imagine how we did it all, but we did, and thrived, and I loved it, until that old familiar spectre of discontent rapped at our door again. It seemed more wilderness was what it would take to assuage this hunger.

It was just at this point that the fireside chat with Robert and Carolyn turned our thinking toward unknown Canada. At the time I suspected this might turn into another mere "chasing of elusive dreams and schemes", but still the prospect was exciting. I remembered the dutiful line: Whither thou goest there shall I go also.

Someone shouted, "Look at the bear!" Immediately I was back in the Canadian wilderness. We'd just rounded a bend in the road when fifty yards ahead of us a big black furry bear stopped in the middle of his crossing, swung his gaze toward us, then ambled on, eager, I suppose, to remove himself from the sound of this noisy caravan intruding on his quiet world of natural solitude. We all wondered how common the bears and other forms of wild animals were going to be. Would they be a problem? But after that little excitement the driving continued on and on, over the dusty dirt road toward the tiny settlement of Manson Creek and our date with destiny.

The four or five hour trip between Fort St. James and Manson Creek can be delightful, or it can be tiring and boring, depending on the current mood of each individual traveler. The most ardent nature lover stands a chance of experiencing periods of lassitude with the miles upon miles of nearly identical scenery. There is always the possibility of seeing a bear or a lynx loping across the road, or a moose galloping awkwardly ahead of the vehicle which startled it. And along the stretch of miles where the road contours the string of Manson Lakes, one is treated to a breathtaking panoramic view of the sky and opposite mountains mirrored in the silent waters.

About the time I was giving up all hope of ever reaching our destination, we suddenly found ourselves going up the last little rise and onto the plateau which supports the town of Manson Creek. Enthusiasm peaked! It was nine o'clock in the evening, but the brightness of the northern sky could have indicated mid-afternoon when we rolled up to this interesting little log-cabin community. The only apparent central feature of town was the building bearing on its roof a roughly hewn "Trading Post" sign, so that's where our trucks came to a halt.

Several young men were lounging casually on the store porch. They smiled in friendly fashion and greeted us as we climbed out. The only sounds in this vast stillness were the muffled roar of the creek and the stopping and starting of a motor on a piece of machinery somewhere out of sight. At first glance "town" seemed to consist of log buildings. Interestingly, some stood on stilts three feet above the ground level. Up the road a few hundred feet was another cabin set off by itself, but surrounded by assorted heavy machinery which obviously must be used for mining. A few men were working over the equipment with welding outfits. So this was what the dot on the map marked Manson Creek looked like!

Robert made the first comment: "Well, there seems to be life here."

Making our way through the long legs of the boys on the porch, we entered the trading post. There behind the counter sat a wiry 75-year-old gentleman talking with three other oldtimers who were perched on makeshift chairs around an unlit barrel stove. The scene was so genuinely "Old West" that one could expect to see pickle crocks, cracker barrels and candy jars full of licorice, horehound and peppermint sticks.

"How-de-do, folks. Glad to see you," volunteered the man behind the counter.

"Mr. Hamilton, I presume?" Larry began. A perceptible nod from the old man indicated he had the right party, so he continued. "I'm Larry Owen and this is my wife, Maggie, and our family. And over there are our friends, Robert and Carolyn Marrs. We've just come from the realty office in Vanderhoof and they told us that your place here is for sale. I have a letter from Mrs. Hobson."

Mr. Hamilton's manner changed momentarily from the casual "welcome to Manson Creek" to one of "proceed with instinctive caution," and for a fleeting instant I was sure he didn't want to sell. Perhaps the sale was being forced on him and he wasn't going to give up easily.

Recovering himself quickly, however, he assumed his habitual guide-to-tourist role saying, "Well now, I see by your license plates that you've come all the way from California."

"That's right. Southern California — Los Angeles area," I replied, filing away in my mind fact number one: that license-plate-noting is a pastime-with-a-purpose in the tourist business.

"How long you been on the road?"

"A week and a half," Larry answered. "We haven't hurried — just looked the country over as we went along, and camped each night on the way."

"Well now, that's a long camping trip with a baby," Mr. Hamilton volunteered.

For the first time, Robert spoke up. "Oh, we've had a good time. We haven't had to hurry and we're well equipped. Everything we own is on the trucks outside."

I sensed the old man wince, as if he suddenly realized that this party really meant business.

"You mean to say that you just packed it all up and headed north without knowing what you were getting into?"

"Right," Bob continued. "We're prepared to build a cabin if we have to. In fact, that's exactly what we'd planned to do in the beginning, until we found out a couple of days ago that lakeshore property isn't for sale in British Columbia."

Mr. Hamilton shook his head sadly. "Young people these days — I just don't know — they never seem to think and plan ahead."

I was getting a bit riled by now. "Mr. Hamilton, we *did* think and plan ahead. We're all outdoorsy people. We camped all the way because we wanted to do it that way, and we're prepared and equipped to build our homes up here. Canada has opened its arms to us, but the Government in its advertising didn't make it at all clear what people can and can't buy in the way of land. We came here to see Manson Creek because you had it for sale, and we're prepared financially to buy this place or anything else we decide we like well enough."

"Well, of course," he said in a slightly mollified tone. "You folks must be tired and there's only a couple of hours of daylight left. Why don't you pitch your tents over there on the flat area? There's a biffy right handy. A mining outfit is working in the creek and muddying up the water, but there's a spring not far away. One of you can come with me and I'll show you the spot. Tomorrow I'll show you around the place."

Just then a resident stuck his head through the doorway and asked for a gallon of naphtha gas.

"O.K., Herb, be right with you," he said, and added for our benefit, "would you folks like to step outside now? I've got to go over to the gas shed."

We all filed out of the store, as did the three old cronies who had remained right where they were through our brief exchange. Mr. Hamilton fumbled with the large assortment of keys attached at the end of his pocket key chain. He locked up the store and we stood outside watching as he walked directly across the dirt road, about fifty feet, to the gas shed, unlocked that padlock, got the gas for Herb, locked the door again, came back across to the store, unlocked the door to go in to make change for the purchase, and came back out, re-locking, and heading over to his own home.

We shook our heads in disbelief. Wasn't this the remote north woods where doors were always left unlocked? There couldn't be more than ten or fifteen people beside ourselves in the immediate area. What was he afraid of?

We Bought the Town!   6

The tents and sleeping bags which had been our homes for the past ten days of travel on the road provided us with another good night's sleep; but this time we awoke to a fresh aspect of the whole adventure. There were sounds of activity in the creek below us, and gazing down from the edge of the thirty-foot embankment we could watch the mining crew at work.

One man operated the back-hoe which took huge chunks of earth, swung the load around and dumped it into the top of a twenty-five-foot-long slanted sluice box which had a rush of water sifting and sorting the load of dirt and rocks all the way down. Another man stationed at the top of the box would push off the larger boulders with a pry-bar, while a "Cat" operator moved the "tailings" out of the way at the bottom. The water pump had constant attention, and that was another crew-member's job. Hopefully, heavy and fine gold was being sifted from the dirt and would be adhering to the "carpet" which ran the length of the sluicebox.

The man who seemed to be in charge was moving around with a goldpan in his hand. Whenever a new area of bed-rock was uncovered he'd grab a pan of the dirt, step aside to some quiet water and pan out the sample, thus making his personal assessment of the newly opened up area. Each of the crew was intent on his own part of the operation and seemed completely unaware of the lineup at the observation post overhead.

"Hey, Carolyn," I half whispered. "Let's go down there and see what the gold panner's doing." She nodded, so we eased away from our group and carefully made our way down the steep path. Actually we were well aware that the game of gold-mining is played very close to the chest, but it didn't seem like intruding to just be friendly. We needn't have given it a thought anyway because the man saw us approaching and called us over.

"Hold out your hands, girls," he said, a warm smile breaking over his ruggedly handsome features. He couldn't have been much over thirty, and with the heavy crop of curly black hair a-top his muscular frame, the total picture suggested a pirate buccaneer rather than our preconceived notion of what gold miners should look like. "Here's a few 'clinkers' for you," he said, dropping three or four tiny chunks of raw gold into each of our hands.

"Gee, really!" we both exclaimed. "Thanks a lot." We both admitted that these were the first gold nuggets we'd ever touched.

"Why do you call them 'clinkers'?" Carolyn asked.

"Because they clink when you drop them in the gold pan. The bigger ones are called 'klunkers.' Can you guess why?" We laughed at his good humor, and he switched subjects abruptly. "I understand that you folks are considering buying Manson. Is that right?"

"Well . . ." Carolyn and I looked at each other dumbfounded. Word surely does get around in a small town. "Well, we came up to look the place over," I said. "We may buy it. Our plans are uncertain as yet."

The rest of our gang soon joined us and there were introductions all around. Our new friend, Tony, talked eagerly and explained all about his mining operation. Things were so lively and friendly that even I forgot for a while that we were so far removed from everything I'd ever known.

Just about then Mr. Hamilton came looking for us and said he was ready to show us around. We left Tony and were ready to concentrate on the guided tour at hand. But first we had to be told in no uncertain terms that we shouldn't have been down there, and that gold miners don't like people getting too close to what they are doing. When Carolyn and I showed him what Tony had given us, he was speechless and just shrugged.

On with the tour . . . Besides the store with its Post Office in the back, there was the main house for the owner, three small rental cabins, a large warehouse for storage, a gas-house with barrels of various types of fuel, a meat-hanging house, and even a rail-fenced little cemetery with about a twelve-grave capacity. The total area of "town" was, and still is, only 2.2 acres, but with all the surrounding wide-open space, no fences, and very few other cabins or homes around, boundaries have little meaning.

There are hills to the south and north of the mile-wide valley. The road winds through and on westerly, then northerly for another seventy miles. At the twenty-mile point on this road is a similar small settlement called Germansen Landing.

After spending a couple of hours talking with Mr. and Mrs. Hamilton, we went back to our tents to confer on whether or not to buy. It wasn't exactly what we originally had in mind, but neither was it too far removed when one considered all the possibilities. If we wanted to, we could build that hoped-for lodge right here in town and advertise for hunters and fishermen. Meanwhile here were our homes already built, and there would be very little expense to living in them. We kept reminding ourselves that there would even be a small income from the store. And the price was so reasonable! There couldn't have been much more than a couple of thousand dollars worth of goods in the Trading Post; but had there been five thousand worth to add onto the sale price, it still would have been a ridiculously good buy. So we did it. We bought Manson Creek! And because settlements are so scarce in the upper two-thirds of the province, most all of them are located and named on most every map. We could hardly wait to check our atlas, but it was packed along with the boxes of books too far forward in one of the trucks. Later on when we had unloaded and settled in, we remembered to look, and there it was, sure'nuff — "Manson Creek" — right in the center of the province of British Columbia. It was a unique feeling to own a place on the map — a town. We wondered what our friends back home would think of that distinction.

The Hamiltons were not in as much of a hurry to move out as we were to move in, and we began what turned into three more weeks of tent-living, with meals cooked and eaten outdoors in the height of the mosquito and black-fly season. We tried to be patient since we were dealing with an elderly couple who were obviously not happy about departing from their home.

At times it seemed they were making it as difficult as possible, hoping we would get fed-up and leave. Several times Larry and Robert were all set to do just that! I take full credit for pouring much of the proverbial oil on many troubled waters, thereby holding our camp together during trying times. The already-built homes in this little town appealed to me right off — far better than the prospect of cutting down trees and starting to clear ground to build our own cabins. Besides that, the lateness of the summer was on my side, too.

I'll have to admit that I couldn't have done it without the help of Tony and his crew, even though Tony, assessing from a Canadian point of view, advised that the property wasn't worth what Mr. Hamilton was asking. He couldn't dissuade us on the basis of the selling price. We Yankees were agreed on one thing — this property was a "steal" compared with what we had just left in California.

During this long wait before we could take over, Tony's camp trailer-kitchen was the scene of much conviviality. We couldn't walk within hailing distance without being invited in for coffee and freshly baked buns, or pie, or goodies of some kind. George, the cook, and Tony were both so congenial. Many times I felt that we should refuse the invitations and let George get his cooking done. But he kept his men fed and happy, and did a tremendous job of it, even under the trying circumstances of our too-frequent presence.

One day Mr. Hamilton said that it was time to take inventory of the stock in the store. We volunteered a generous offer in estimate form, but he insisted it must be done properly and requested Carolyn and me to help. He gave us each a large legal-sized tablet of paper, and there were to be two records, hopefully identical. We were told to both write down the items, the quantity of each, and the cost, as he called out the information. Being oriented in the big city way of speed and efficiency, computers and calculators, we were totally unprepared for Mr. Hamilton's method of stock-taking. He removed each row of canned goods, counted the items, and put them back into place before the next row was taken down. We could see to count them before he even took them down, but this was his show. Every pound of nails was weighed. Every grain of rice went into the scales, as did each loose bean or pea. No estimates were allowed. There wasn't a single screw, nut, bolt, old dusty bottle of medicine — absolutely nothing under the store roof — which escaped being handled, listed, priced, and totaled in.

It took four days to do the inventory, working a few hours each afternoon; and after that came the figuring. Mr. Hamilton took one copy of the list to his house, and we took the other to our tents. Each item on the sheaf of pages had to be multiplied out, and each page totaled without benefit of adding machines. With four of us to share the work, we were finished in a very short while; but the lamps burned long into the small hours for two nights until Mr. Hamilton had his listings totaled. When we got together again, theoretically our page totals should have matched, but naturally they didn't. When all the problems were discovered and all the corrections made, the grand total came out to exactly $240.00 less than Larry's original offer in estimate form — much to Mr. Hamilton's chagrin and our concealed amusement.

Also during that seemingly interminable three weeks' wait for the owners to leave, we took a very necessary trip back to Prince George to declare ourselves and our possessions and begin the "Landed Immigrant" proceedings. We went armed with lists of all our household belongings and tools, and all the motor and serial numbers of vehicles and equipment. The paperwork was easy and not too time-consuming. Physical examinations and chest X-rays were also required and were accomplished painlessly in a couple of days. When we headed back to Manson Creek it was with the hope that the Hamiltons were ready to leave. No such luck. Not yet.

To while away another day we took a trip to investigate the neighboring town of Germansen Landing, about eighteen miles farther along the road. What a delightful surprise to meet the Westfall family there! They had come to Canada from Idaho the previous year and were enthusiastic about their new life. Their three children were all within a two-year age range of our girls. There was one daughter, Amy, and two boys, Keith and Kim.

Glenn, more familiarly called "Wes", and his wife, Maggie (here were two American Maggies in such a sparsely populated area!) own a large area of land on the south bank of the Omineca River which flows through town. They have a lovely, comfortable two-storey home, a small trading post much like the one at Manson, a few rental cabins, and a weather station. Electronics had been Wes's vocation during the war, and it is still an eagerly pursued avocation. His radio room houses several different radio-phones, testing equipment, batteries, and other paraphernalia quite incomprehensible to the casual observer. The weather station is a family project and every three hours, day and night, every day of the week, reports of the charts, meters and gauges are radioed in. Westfalls also have direct radio connections to the airline offices in Prince George and in the Fort. It is their duty and privilege to assist pilots flying overhead or making a landing or take-off in the river out front.

Mr. Westfall's ready sense of humor and good supply of appropriate anecdotes made for a delightful visit. Discovering this happy family was one of those little surprises that kept happening to us.

Directly across the river lived Don and Irene Gilliland. They, too, had a small store, several guest cabins and a cafe which was set up in the living room and kitchen of their home during the tourist season. Don was a big-game guide for American hunters who come up in the fall. They invited us in for coffee and cookies and enlightened us further about what the life up here had to offer. Each of the buildings on their property was of log construction and had been masterfully put up over a period of many years. Don and Irene had done all the work together, and they could well be proud of their craftsmanship.

On the homeward trip, the last stop was at Gene Jack's mining camp two miles back toward Manson. This area had been the site of a very successful gold mining operation which was active back in the "thirties". Gene had picked up the leases five years ago and with the help of a few men he worked the mine periodically and sometimes profitably.

Gene's wife, Betty, a temporarily retired schoolteacher, his two teenage sons Doug and Steve, and small daughter Sharon, all occupied the main house on the property. The rest of the camp consisted of cabins for workers, a large shop boasting an enviable supply of spare new parts for repairing just about any type of equipment, a few warehouses, garages, a hangar for Gene's small plane, and a stable for the two horses. There was even a 1600-foot airstrip on the adjacent property. Our total reaction was: Wow, what a country! We weren't going to be all that alone here after all. Without a doubt that mileage between Manson and Germansen would be traveled frequently.

Finally we Moved in 7

Back at Manson we waited day after day until eventually the time for the Hamiltons' departure had arrived. Just as soon as their truckload of belongings rounded the bend leaving town we began the big move in. Bob and Carolyn set up housekeeping in one of the cabins. Our larger family took over the main house.

Carolyn had accepted the job of Postmistress, and I wound up with storekeeper responsibilities. Assistance behind the counter was guaranteed whenever it should become necessary, but that was really a laugh because during the first couple of years, only a few cars would drive through each day. Lyn and Les thought it great fun to play store for real with genuine money, genuine merchandise, and real live paying customers. With due caution we let Lyn take over the store for short intervals. She caught on readily to the making of change, and could easily handle the quick trips of the local residents for a dozen eggs, a pack of cigarettes, or whatever.

Larry and Robert were not assigned specific jobs, but were active in the public-relations department and the planning of future development. These were time-consuming operations since a basic requirement in getting minds and wits sharpened for action was to keep the coffee pot busy at all times, or better still, the neighbors' pots. In between times they did some roof and cabin repairing, woodcutting for the next winter, and were generally indispensable around town.

This kind of life and leisure was new and different to all of us. There were short walks to survey surrounding areas, all sorts of investigating by the girls, and much distracted watching of the wanderings of our little toddler, Evy. He really moved around, and with no particular objectives in mind beyond moving. One time, after a frantic ten minutes' search on all his usual routes, we found him following a white cat through the bushes not far away. (We saw the cat before we saw Evy.)

After this particular episode, our bachelor neighbor up the road volunteered a big brass cow-bell on a wide leather strap to hang around Evy's neck so we'd always know where he was. To this day, as well as I know Johnny, I'll never know whether that cowbell offering was a joke, a mild reprimand that we should have known better than to bring a tiny kid up into the wilderness, or whether he seriously thought Evy would leave the heavy object hanging around his neck. At any rate, we didn't hang it in the intended place. We resolved to keep a better eye on Evy and hung the bell on the outside of the store door. There it still hangs to this day, and summons us whenever someone has arrived at the store without us having noticed.

Each day we'd meet someone we hadn't known the day before, be they resident or tourist. We made the most of every opportunity to make friends with anyone passing through. From recent first-hand experience, we knew that each car stopping at the store had passengers who must be weary of the long drive and ready to pause in their travels to refresh themselves. We poured on the charm as we poured cups of coffee and engaged in animated conversations. A guest book was started immediately to acquire names and addresses of people whom we really enjoyed and might like to send Christmas greetings to in the dead of winter.

The wife of one of the hunters we entertained asked me if we were keeping a journal or diary. "You could write a book someday about your experiences here," she suggested.

That was the day I started the first book of reminiscences which was a combination diary, scrapbook, journal and photo album, kept in looseleaf notebook form. The idea was so successful that there is a fat, full notebook for each year we've been at Manson. Over the years these books began taking on almost official proportions. They have been referred to by our freight men, Royal Canadian Mounted Police officers looking for a happening on some certain date, and by people in the area who for some reason needed to know just when something occurred or someone arrived in town. On many an occasion members of the family would pull out one of the books to prove a point or to just sit and thumb through it for some laughs or happy rememberings. In a convoluted sort of fashion, it was the local newspaper — without circulation.

Hunting season, beginning in the fall, brought a spate of vehicles and people which none of us expected. It was a reassuring feeling to realize that maybe this deserted spot wasn't so deserted after all.

Occasionally people would ask if we served meals or if there was a restaurant around. The answer to both questions was negative, but there were times when it would seem that we were doing someone a real service to respond with a casual offer of potluck with the family. On one of these times we entertained two men — brothers — who had come up on a hunting trip. The drive had been much longer than they had anticipated or were prepared for, and they were exhausted and hungry. During the course of the meal, the conversation revealed that we had a college president (from Nebraska) in our midst. Needless to say, Larry and I were impressed. I, personally, kept realizing that people — and most of them very interesting people — *do* come up this long road, and for a great variety of reasons.

One day while Westfalls were visiting at Manson, a man wearing a torn coat appeared at the door looking slightly distraught. He calmly told us that in attempting a landing on Gene Jack's airstrip he'd crash-landed his plane. Horses grazing on the runway had spooked at the sound of the approaching plane, and in the resulting confusion the aircraft ended up in the trees. It was a masterful, or lucky crash-land, however, because there had been no fire and only a minimum of scratches and bruises, although the plane was a total loss.

But when this gentleman first came to the door, my reaction was, "Good grief, what a small world!" Here we were in this vast new country, not knowing a soul in advance, and already we were seeing so unexpectedly someone we had met and talked with two months earlier and two-hundred miles away. This fact was more impressive to me than the more immediate fact of his present distress. He was the Government Land Agent whom we had consulted in Prince George before we ever saw Manson Creek. He had kindly offered to obtain some information by telegram for us. While awaiting the reply we had sat in his office and conversed about our life back in Southern California and our hopes for the new beginning in Canada. Now he had dropped in on us out of the sky. Small world, indeed!

Manson Creek wasn't anywhere near as desolate as I had thought while we were driving up that dirt road the first time. Things were looking excitingly better day by day. Maybe we had done the right thing after all, in buying this remote speck on the map, with the idea of developing it. Of the four of us adults I had had the longest way to go in total acceptance of what we were doing, but already I was much happier about the whole thing.

So busy were we getting settled in at Manson that we had little to think about the colorful past of the mining camp. We knew it had come into existence many years before, was at times virtually a ghost town and had been given new but small scale renewal of population and ambition by occasional revivals of mining and prospecting along with the always reliable activities of trapping and fur trading.

Later we were to learn, from Bruce Ramsey's Ghost Towns of British Columbia and other sources, that the Camp's first discovery of gold was credited to a certain Robert Howell, who had come to British Columbia in the early 1860's with the Royal Corps of Engineers. He, with his red-coated comrades, had been engaged in the building of the famous Cariboo wagon road to the equally celebrated Cariboo gold fields centered on Barkerville.

Gold seekers from all over the world tried their luck on the Cariboo Creeks. Those who came too late or were just unlucky in their diggings moved on northward. Howell, who had resigned from the Engineers, discovered gold on Manson Creek and three gold camps developed in the years 1869 to 1871 — Manson, Dunkeld and Howelltown. Only Manson had survived.

If we were happy with the prospect presented by Manson Creek, not so had been H. H. Bancroft, the pioneer Northwest traveler and historian, who saw the place in its gold diggings hey-dey and wrote: "Saloons, cards, fur traders, miners and Hydah squaws for *genre;* ditch drains, log cabins and stick forest for scenery — these made up what was regarded as the somewhat miserable picture of the town of Manson Creek."

Obviously Bancroft was no real estate promotion man.

The creek gravels yielded gold but not in appreciable amounts. But the cabins remained, trappers, miners and prospectors, sometimes in considerable numbers, gratefully sheltered there and a trading post usually afforded supplies. Manson stayed on the map and this was what we had bought — including, we observed, a decidedly dilapidated community graveyard!

Business of Getting Acquainted 8

Daily life immediately began to fall into a pattern, the main feature of the pattern being "expect the unexpected." New and different things were happening every day with new and different people. My journal-scrapbook was growing with entries. Never had life been so full and active. Our home was something resembling a perpetual open-house party.

Each day after breakfast Carolyn and Robert would come over. We'd talk over the day's work plan, drink coffee, and then wander out into the brisk, beautifully clear air of our 3000-foot-high valley. Probably by this time the first car would have driven up to the store. Its occupants would pile out, stretch their muscles in relieved fashion, take a look around and begin gravitating towards the store. No one was ever in a hurry so we'd stroll over and become acquainted through the very human art of conversation. If the people seemed interesting and the talk was easy, we'd invite them over to the house for coffee. Work could always wait. Many work-hours were set aside for pleasure over the coffee cups. Occasionally overnight guests would rent our cabins, and after they'd settled in and eaten a meal, they'd almost invariably stroll around outside to enjoy the extended bright twilight. That would lead to more talk and more coffee. There really wasn't much else for them to do of an evening. There was then, and still is, nothing in the form of commercial entertainment at Manson.

In addition to all the tourists, we were frequently meeting some other resident whom we hadn't realized was around. It took a while to explore up and down all the winding sideroads and locate the few hidden away cabins. Five miles up the creek lived a trapper and his Indian wife. Down a road branching off the main road there were three or four cabins which housed bachelors all of whom had done, or were still doing, a bit of gold mining. Around a few more curves on that same sideroad was a cabin with a few outbuildings belonging to a couple who would come up from Vancouver each summer to work their placer claim. Our only near neighbors were two gentlemen, both retired miners, and both living in their separate cabins only a stone's throw from us. Down by Wolverine Lake, three miles distant, lived two Indian families — sometimes. They seemed to gravitate between Wolverine Lake and Fort St. James. I never did find out which place they considered home.

Zooming back and forth through town several times a day was a very busy lady-miner. It took longer to get to know her because she was always in a hurry and just didn't have time for coffee and idle chatter. We got the immediate impression that she was someone of great importance in the mining field because she had claims on just about all the property up and down the two creeks surrounding us, as well as on other creeks and rivers farther away. She was always either expecting some mining engineer in to look at a property, or else already had someone in testing some of her ground.

One morning we awoke to what sounded like the jingle of cow bells. Outside the window stood six horses grazing on the late summer grasses. We met their owner later in the day when he came looking for them. He was a bouncy, twenty-three year old young fellow who had already attained the status of Big Game Hunting Guide and who was now in the process of buying, from the man he had worked and trained with, the guiding territory thirty miles west of us, and all the horses, equipment, and cabins that went with it.

The wandering horses had strayed away from camp and had started down the road towards Fort St. James. This was an habitual trek of theirs because each year after the hunting season is over, the horses are encouraged to walk and graze their way back to the Fort where they spend the winter. The fact that the horses do get there without losing their way, or without being mistakenly shot for moose, amazed us.

The horses' owner impressed us immediately. He was such a boisterous individual, laughing and enthusiastic about everything. He seemed to know his horses and his business so well that we could predict nothing but success for him in his new venture.

Any other residents we hadn't met yet, we became acquainted with on the day of a Provincial election. Manson Creek had been designated as a polling place, and the twelve legitimate voters of the Manson-Germansen areas drifted in throughout the day.

Tony's mining crew were still at work down in the creek during this time of our getting settled and learning to know the people and the area. Being the eager-beaver hunter of our outfit, Robert was grumbling about the six-months' residency rule which would prohibit him from shooting a moose until after December, and by then the hunting season would be over. But no such rule stood in Tony's way, and for a week or so he'd take Robert along with him every sun-up and sun-down until a beautiful young bull moose was brought down. Tony and Robert hauled it back to camp, strung it up by the hind feet, using the D-8 Cat winch, and set to work skinning and gutting the eight-hundred pound animal. It was a gory, grisly sight there in the night, with truck headlights playing on the scene. Neither Larry nor I had had any hunting experience at all, so this was all new and revolting to me. I guess it didn't bother Larry too much, but I was slightly queasy watching the head being sawn off, and thought I should remove the kids from the scene. They were engrossingly absorbed, however, and not in the least horrified. Of course, after a few more experiences like this I became a bit more mature, but that first time was gruesome.

This was Tony's moose, so he announced that after the meat had hung a few days he would cut it into as many steaks as the carcass would yield and there would be a barbecue for everyone. The date was set and verbal announcements spread among the local residents.

Just before the big picnic, Tony and his wife (she had come in for the last week of the mining operation) marinated the steaks overnight. Next day the pit was dug to specifications, the huge wood fire was burned down to the just-right stage of coals, and a grill welded together from bits and pieces of metal was placed over it. Tony's cook, George, baked pans and pans of buns and brewed huge pots of coffee. Carolyn and I rounded up the biggest tub we could find for potato salad. Someone told us about an ice-well a couple of miles away, so while we got out the fixin's for ice cream, and the hand-crank freezer we'd brought with us, the fellows and kids went off in the truck to chop some ice from the special sheltered hole in the ground.

The charcoal-broiled moose steaks surpassed all expectations. Of the twenty-five people assembled, we newcomers were the only ones who had never tasted moosemeat, and we had no idea it could be so delicious. I'm not sure we've ever had it so tasty since, but charcoal-broiled was the perfect introduction. And the ice cream — even though we couldn't wait for it to freeze properly — was a most appropriate top-off. The old-timers present remarked again and again that Manson Creek had never been like this in the past twenty years.

Larry and Robert were both healthy, muscular outdoorsmen and adapted immediately to this new way of life. Robert, the mechanic-builder of the two, was called upon for all sorts of car problems, and Larry fixed many a flat tire. It's amazing the number of cars and trucks that develop problems after driving so far over a dirt road.

Lyn and Les were busy all day every day exploring every hidden spot within a radius of a quarter-mile. Slate Creek meandering through the narrow valley behind our home provided the most attractions. Beaver dams had backed up the water, creating grassy ponds. Fingers of streams trickled out from pond fringes and created miniature waterfalls, little rivulets, and small islands. All this was made even more intriguing by the willows, spruce trees and poplars which provided shaded areas and hiding places. The girls whiled away many happy, contented hours in this paradise which they thought was their very own. Unfortunately, a few years later all of us almost shed tears when an unfeeling back-hoe and tractor ripped up this parkland on a relentless surge of busy-work called, in mining lingo, "assessment work." When it was over, all one could see was acres of a raw, bare scar on the earth's surface. We called it "the desecration of Slate Creek" but the busy lady-miner informed us in no uncertain terms that this was mining country, and Progress Must Go On!

Evy spent his days poking around in the dirt, making roads for his little trucks, happily occupied all day as only two-year-olds can be. We eventually had to instigate a rigid training program with him because he kept wandering off aimlessly and although not too far away from the house, still he would be out of sight. The punishment was firm and was meted out frequently enough that he caught on rather quickly. A fenced-in yard would have accomplished the same thing more easily, but Evy learned.

A visitor from Fort St. James suggested that we could use a dog here and we half agreed. He said that there was a beautiful eight-month-old German Shepherd pup available and that it was a good, well-bred dog, but had been teased and tormented through its fence to the point of having bitten a few people. There were orders for the dog to be destroyed if it wasn't removed from its present location.

As I said, we only half agreed, and then proceeded to forget the whole incident. A week later, on Thanksgiving Day (in Canada this holiday occurs in October) a car full of young boys and a huge dog drove into town.

"We have your dog here," they called across the road.

Out of the car jumped a hundred-pound monster on a long rope leash. We all retreated several steps in shocked disbelief. The boys said his name was "King." Although not an original name, it certainly was appropriate. King was a golden wheat-coloured, healthy, huge-headed horse of a dog.

Robert took the lead in getting acquainted. He took the leash cautiously, patted King, and talked to him. After a bit he untied the leash and let King run. Off went the dog with tremendous strides, round and round the store, and several times around the house. When Bob called him he came at once. "Good dog, good dog!"

Next came the dishes of food and water, both of which were gulped down with enthusiasm.

Carolyn and I kept the kids and ourselves at a distance, just as a precaution. The rest of the afternoon we kept King tied on the long rope in case he shouldn't realize that here was his new home. He seemed gentle and friendly enough, but just the size of the beast was enough to frighten anyone. That night we put a mat on the floor and let him sleep in the house. Next day, with all the attention he was getting, it didn't seem necessary to tie King up — nor ever again. He took to us all readily and has been no problem all these years, with only a few minor exceptions. He has been the target of many comments from strangers because of his unusual size and coloring. King was notably a handsome dog.

Living and Working Quarters 9

When we made up our minds that Manson Creek was what we wanted, it certainly wasn't because of the beauty of the home we were moving into. One of our loveliest residences in Southern California had been a sprawling ranch-type home on acreage surrounded by orange and avocado orchards. We lived there for two years — just long enough to do a professional-looking landscape job on the 120-foot frontage of yard (which was all that had been lacking in this completely carpeted, patioed, luxurious home and property), and then re-sold it, as we'd done with a few other residences.

But of course we weren't looking for anything remotely related to this type of luxury in the Canadian north woods. As a matter of fact, after living out of trucks and tents for a month and a half, anything — just anything — was welcome. Actually the house we moved into was much more than merely a roof over our heads. It was a log construction, twenty-five feet square. The inside walls were paneled with a soft, fibrous wallboard and a dividing wall down the center made a long 12 by 25-foot living room-kitchen combination. The other half was divided again into two bedrooms.

When we first saw the house furnished with the Hamiltons' belongings, it looked extremely cosy, friendly and warm. After they left with their furniture, pictures, knick-knacks, and trimmings, however, we saw the place in its true colors which were bright pea-green where the pictures had been and faded, smoky pea-green on the rest of the walls. An all-over floral patterned linoleum covered the entire floor and was in fair condition except for a few badly worn paths in the traveled areas. Windows were trimmed in assorted types and colors of fabric and fiber. The total effect was challenging.

Furniture consisted of a bed and dresser in each bedroom. A large homemade, all-purpose wooden table, a few assorted chairs, an old-fashioned metal-frame daybed which served as a sofa, and an adequate wood heater comprised the living room ensemble. The kitchen boasted a large wood-stove, a shelf for water buckets and wash basin, an open cupboard for dishes, and nails on the wall for hanging pots and pans. Toilet facilities of course, were the rustic "little brown shack" type, and it was obvious that the largest galvanized tub we could locate was going to serve as a bathtub.

A white enamel wringer washing-machine, housed in the spare room at the back of the house, was a special delight for Carolyn and me since we'd expected we'd have to scrub-board our laundry. It was a gasoline-powered machine and Mr. Hamilton had demonstrated how the motor was started by pumping a foot pedal. Hanging on the wall near the washer were two copper boilers for heating the wash water. They were oval shaped, 12″ wide, 22″ long, and 12″ high, with handles on both ends for lifting and carrying. Larry and I were amazed at how frequently we were learning about new and different ways of doing things. Actually they weren't "new" methods and tools at all, but just completely foreign to city people. Bob and Carolyn had a slight advantage over us since both had been born and reared in farm surroundings where these things were commonplace.

A small generator was housed out behind the woodshed. It carried enough direct current to run the 12-volt lighting system around town, but would not power any appliances or machinery using alternating current. We accepted the role of private power utility providers without being overly impressed by its importance.

Well . . . this was to be home for a while. We'd have to do a lot of fixing up, but having planned originally to build a home from "scratch" and build all our furniture, this humble abode was giving us a head start.

The three rental cabins were 18- by 20-foot one-room log structures. Each had a single and double bed (old-fashioned iron frames with springs and stuffed mattresses), a table, a few chairs, dishes, pans, utensils and a wood stove for cooking as well as for heat. The furnishings were surprisingly adequate for rental cabins, but the one thing that kept catching my eye was the assortment of window-trimmings. I couldn't help feeling that if the three windows in any one cabin all had matching curtains, the interiors of the buildings would be far more pleasing to the eye. Such a simple thing; but all these minor details would have to be attended to later.

The store being the main attraction of town commanded our first and most enthusiastic attention. It had been built in 1936 by the famous old Hudson's Bay Company, and had been one of their outposts until sometime during World War II. Since then there had been several private owners. In its early days it was one of two stores in the area serving about three-hundred people! (Consolidated Mining and Smelting Company, referred to locally as "C.M. & S.", had had a producing gold mine about three miles from town, and their employees accounted for most of the total population. Incidentally, Consolidated's old dilapitated buildings, the tailings piles, and the rusty equipment are now tourist attractions.)

Inside the store, floor-space is about 20 by 30 feet — all one big room except for a partial divider at the back which allows for storage on one side and the Post Office on the other. Shelves line the store walls and a few tables display special items. The floor boards were buckling a little, and the whole building had obviously settled because the shelves were noticeably slanted and the door wouldn't close properly. During the first winter Robert and Larry did some jacking-up of the shelf structures, thereby improving on the tipsy angles a bit. As with other things around the place, a new store building would be in order some day.

When we took over in August we knew that the summer season was pretty well over, but there was still the moose hunter influx to look forward to until late October. Mr. Hamilton had informed us that Manson Creek's tourist business is nothing great, but the hunting season is something entirely different. With this in mind, we set about ordering new items which might go over well, rearranged things on the shelves, and in general did over the store to suit our taste.

Having been avid super-market shoppers in Southern California, we found the comparison of store items and prices amusing as well as startling. As for prices, if you've ever been to any small, remote mountain store and been horrified at the price of groceries, you'll have an idea of the cost of a can of peaches here. It's assumed that everyone knows it costs money to truck-freight goods up mountain roads. The thing we didn't realize at first and what most people probably never think about, is that any storekeeper in a remote area who has a small "turn-over" has his money tied up in stock for a longer time than does the average store owner, and is thereby entitled, by gentlemen's agreement, to a higher mark-up.

Mr. Hamilton's small supply of store goods consisted of canned goods, dried staple items, a shelf of drug-sundries, tobaccos, a few shelves of hardware items, and a small supply of dry-goods. As we studied the merchandise more closely we were frequently amused by some of the quaint items we discovered. Only casual survey was given to the fruits, vegetables, meats, soups, juices and other canned and packaged goods. What intrigued us first were the deep drawers in the big old desk-counter which were filled with rice, pearl tapioca, dried peas, white beans and kidney beans. Being basically thrifty, we couldn't just toss out all this loose merchandise, so we decided to wait and see how

38

the bulk goods would sell. But by the next summer we had found more suitable containers for the legumes and more appropriate uses for the desk drawers.

The drug shelves contained the usual first aids, aspirin, hair goods, teeth and shaving needs, but we also found all sorts of little bottles and tubes of ointment for piles, toothache remedies, kidney and liver pills, and cures for everything from diarrhea to constipation. This was going to be fun; we would modernize Manson Creek Trading Post. Out with the old, in with the new! Well, when it came right down to throwing merchandise into the trash can, we hesitated again. Instead of discarding them, we moved the undesirable goods into less prominent locations and again decided to await eventualities. This time we were surprised. People up here *do* buy these old-fashioned remedies. And on second thought, it makes sense that living such a distance from a doctor, people learn to have faith in a medication which they've been using effectively for years and years. So . . . the little tubes and bottles came back to their rightful places.

The tobacco department featured not only cigarettes and cigars but assorted half-pound cans of fine-cut tobacco and the little packages of cigarette papers for the "roll your own" advocates. It didn't take long to discover that most fellows living up here do just that. Back home when we were preparing to come to Canada, Robert had somewhere acquired a little hand gadget for rolling cigarettes. He bought a pouch of tobacco and a package of papers, and proceeded to give us a demonstration. We were all duly amazed, and since there were three smokers in our prospective party, we wisely decided to take this small piece of equipment along. With our future location uncertain, we might find ourselves too remote to be able to keep commercial cigarettes properly over a long winter. In Canada we discovered that people really do "roll 'em" for real, and not just in old Western movies.

Also prominent on the tobacco shelves were cans of plug tobacco — both chewing and smoking varieties — and snuff. Amongst many of the old timers snuff seems to be a staple item.

Moving to the dry-goods section, we found a supply of gloves of all types, but of only one size. Work gloves, rubber gloves, leather gloves, mitts, mitt liners all came in "Men's Large". The work sox were all size 11, but they were graded commercially in 5-pound, 3½-pound and 2½-pound. We had to have this interpreted, and were told that the heaviest wool socks weigh five pounds per dozen pairs. Next grade — four pounds per dozen, then 3½ pounds, and on down to 2½ pounds. Well, we were out to learn, and we certainly were learning.

On the dry goods shelves there were also a few work shirts, dress shirts, long-johns, assorted boxer shorts up to size 46, one pair of ladies' shoes, and one man's felt hat size 5½.

The small assortment of hardware items were contained on only a few shelves, but there was a plentiful supply of nails of all sizes for building, and all in their separate, special bins.

Mr. Hamilton had now and then acquired an overabundance of some items, so the surplus stock was kept across the road in the warehouse-on-stilts. There were six or seven one-hundred pound sacks of flour in a wooden crate. A screened cage had two slabs of bacon hanging inside. Mr. Hamilton had shown us the "wilderness method" of keeping down the mold on bacon during the hot summer months without refrigeration. Every few days the outside surfaces of the slab must be rubbed down with vinegar. This seemed a pretty neat trick, but in the back of our minds was the idea of a refrigerator for the store, which would first require a different generator. We had only optimistic plans for the future of Manson Creek, envisioning cold drinks being sold in the store, and maybe even ice cream! We'd have to do a lot of serious thinking and planning with the freighter where ice cream was concerned, however.

The gas and oil shed was a headache, but still a most important part of this whole operation. The shed contained two 45-gallon drums of car gas, and one drum each of kerosene and white gas (naphtha) for use in Coleman stoves and lamps. There were cases of car oil of various weights, and chain-saw oil. For dispensing the fuel there was a hand pump, a couple of five-gallon cans, a one-gallon spout can used as a measure, funnels, and small hand tools for opening gas drums and oil cans. A sign on the door in huge letters read: NO SMOKING! The floor of the gas shed was thoroughly soaked from decades of fuel slopping, and it wasn't difficult to imagine what a carelessly thrown match or cigarette could set off!

Whenever a customer drove up for gas, we'd summon Bob or Larry to go through the tedious process of pumping a five-gallon can full of gas, then pouring it through a funnel into the waiting vehicle. This method worked fine until one day when neither of the fellows was around. Carolyn and I struggled with the heavy, awkward pump and then lifted the slopping can over to the car. We were immensely relieved when the obliging driver offered to pour it in. We used this antique method of gas delivery the first year since it was all there was, but we had mental plans for an underground tank and a standing pump for the next year.

That season we went through six or eight 45-gallon drums of gas. It hardly seemed prudent to invest in a 1000-gallon underground tank, but on the other hand, one must always look to the future. No decision was required at the moment and we felt that when it had to be made we'd understand our subject better. But that first year it was a real problem knowing how much gas to have on hand. We were forever running out, but somehow no one was ever stranded for long due to our lack of gas. If we were completely out and the people were in a hurry, we'd suggest the only other possibility which was Germansen Landing and twenty extra miles both ways. It seemed that inexplicably everyone wasn't out of gas at the same time, unless it was a day or two before the freight man was due in.

And the freight trips — that was something else. We had no phone or radio-phone connections with the freighter in Fort St. James, so we never knew for sure when he was coming. He was heard to say at one time that he never came in with less than a full load, so sometimes we'd wait two weeks, or even three. At any rate, each time he did come in we would give him our gas and grocery order for the next trip. Making up these orders in advance was exceedingly difficult, because we just weren't familiar enough with our buying public to know what we'd be out of a few weeks hence.

One thing we observed was that many drivers — indeed, the majority — carried their own spare gas, and we couldn't blame them. It's a long road in, and just as long back out, and cars just don't run without fuel. Before hunting season was over that first year, we had the feeling that a large underground tank for the next year would be advisable.

$2000 Worth of Groceries   10

It was fast approaching October. Our first winter in the wilderness was right around the corner. We did a lot of talking to the old-timers in the area and to anyone with experience, about what we should be doing to prepare for the half year of isolation. The fire-wood supply was in. The house seemed to be adequately chinked to keep out the cold. We guessed that when the winter freeze actually came on, we'd know just where the cold-leak spots were and could then stuff in more chinking as required. We'd heard that clear, heavy plastic tacked over the windows on the outside would provide the equivalent of a double window with an air space, thus keeping the glass from icing up, as well as providing an added measure of warmth. So the plastic had been ordered.

The one big remaining chore was to make up the winter grocery order. There would be no freighting over the road from late October until late in May the next year, so we had to do some realistic planning. There would be the seven of us, plus about six other residents buying from the store during this period, and to find out what items people would be using in quantity seemed to be impossible. We needed more experience with our store and its patrons. In desperation Carolyn and I sat down and went to work with guesses. After many sheets of paper and much pencil-sharpening, we came up with what looked like about $2000 worth of goods! We tried to order wisely — not too much of anything unnecessary, and enough of essentials. A few frills were added which might brighten up otherwise dreary days: nuts, chocolate chips, glacé fruits and hard Christmas candies for the holidays, olives, sweetened condensed milk for special type cooking, popping corn, gum, and canned pie fillings.

The mountain of food which was delivered and stacked inside the store was staggering to us who had never done more than a week's shopping at one time. For three days we were filling shelves, cellars and stockrooms with four hundred pounds each of flour and sugar in 25, 10 and 5 pound sacks (we weren't too sure about the age and condition of the cache of flour in the warehouse), twelve cases (48 per case) of canned milk, 200 lbs. skim milk powder (we had all learned to like skim milk since fresh milk was impossible this far away), a 50-pound can of powdered whole milk, 150 lbs. coffee, 15 cases (15 dozen per case) of eggs, 50 cans of tobacco, and one or two cases each of all the canned meats, fruits, vegetables, etc., in the store. Into the outdoor cold storage box went ten slabs of bacon (about 80 lbs.), two turkeys, 15 chicken fryers, two whole hams and a few rolls of bologna.

The winter was begun with lots of onions, cabbage, carrots, apples and oranges, and that was the extent of our fresh produce. The fruit was gone by January, and from then on we consumed canned fruit for the rest of winter. The vegetables lasted nicely until April and were appreciated.

We had ordered twenty 100-pound sacks of potatoes, after consulting with people who should know. By the following spring we had to toss out about 600 pounds, after giving away all we could force on the residents. That was the only big goof-up in our food ordering that first year.

We'd been told that eggs should be kept at an even temperature and a little above freezing, and also that the crates should be turned upside down faithfully every two weeks. So down in the cellar went fourteen of the fifteen cases, and without fail, every first and fifteenth of each month we turned them over. To our pleased surprise, the eggs kept very well until around the first of March. From then on we began noticing frequent spoiled ones in the thirty dozen which were still left. By the middle of March an egg-sorting day was absolutely necessary and was a never-to-be-forgotten experience. Those which looked dark through the shells were tossed into the dump. The doubtful ones were broken open and either discarded or saved in a bowl for future use. For a joke we broke one into King's dish and he lapped it up with great relish. So King benefited from a lot of half-good eggs. We attempted to use the remaining presumably good ones in cooking, but a stale egg takes on a strange flavour. Attempting to hide it in highly spiced or chocolate cakes or cookies was a wasted effort. The taste was there! We were defeated with the last ten dozen, so we had the last half of March, and April and May to operate in an egg-less fashion. Trying to dream up interesting breakfasts for a family of breakfast-egg eaters was something else. But it wasn't demoralizing and actually we thought we'd done remarkably well having kept them for as long as we did.

Eggs weren't the only shortage. By early spring other evidence of inadequate ordering began showing up. All butter, margarine, and shortenings were being rationed to last a few more months. The store customers were buying only a pound or two at a time so we didn't mention rationing to them. It was in our own usage that we began cutting down drastically. Bread, which requires very little shortening in the making, was getting even less of it. We began exploring the versatility of the prepared biscuit mixes (which the store had lots of) because the shortening was already in them. Toast and bread were spread with peanut-butter or jam or cheese, and baked potatoes no longer were topped with a big gob of butter. Instead we made melted cheese toppings or cream sauces using bacon fat for shortening.

Needless to say, we were somewhat taken aback when Jack the trapper, and his wife, Winnie, asked to buy ten pounds of butter during one of their twice-monthly mail and shopping trips to town. I gulped and asked if five pounds would suffice since our supply was running dreadfully low. They hesitated and then agreed that five pounds would help. I was extremely curious since there seemed to be some specific reason for the quantity, other than for the usual kitchen use. It wasn't until the next fall's hunting season when we were listening to Winnie explain about how she prepared and smoked moosehide for leather-work, that it all became clear. She told how the brains and other innards of the animal were used and at what point the butter was rubbed in! Carolyn and I looked at each other at the same moment. Butter for tanning moosehide! There were hopelessly understanding glances between us as we remembered the tight rationing of the previous winter.

We did have to mention to the residents to go easy on tobacco because it became obvious that we were going to run out and there were so many smokers.

Along with the April mail plane came one of our residents who had been out for the winter and was returning early for the summer season. We were happy to see him again, of course, but his unexpected arrival threw me into a minor panic, for the next day he came to the store to stock up his kitchen again. He was a little disgruntled at all the things we were short of, or out of completely. I stood there behind the counter writing out his bill as things were picked off the shelf — things I'd been hoping would last us through until the end of May. Well, we'd all have to pull the ration strings a little tighter.

That day in the store, he said something which I'v never forgotten: "Shortening and tobacco are two things you should *always* order more of than you think you'll need. You should never run out of those essentials, especially way up here and in winter."

Somehow I'm sure that if we'd been out of sugar and potatoes, his comment would have been: "Sugar and potatoes are two things you should never run out of in bush country."

I took consolation in the fact that for our lack of experience we'd done quite well at keeping food in the mouths of everyone. Next year we'd do lots better.

And, as events were to prove, we did. There is no teacher as effectual as experience. We could order short for the first year, but we could hardly be excused a second time.

A Different Kind of Green Stuff 11

Since northern British Columbia is predominantly mining country, a large percentage of the people we meet here are involved with mining in one way or another. This being so, it seemed inevitable that we, too, would somehow get into the act. And that's just what we did.

It started out with our gold-miner friend Tony, who, one day before he left Manson, took Larry and Robert over to Kwanika Creek (fifty miles west of us) which he had tested and found to be gold-producing. He had previously staked two placer claims there, but since his operation on the Manson had been unsuccessful and he was pulling out crews and equipment from the country, he said that the fellows were welcome to these two Kwanika claims. He had shown them how and where to set up a small sluice box and have some fun each summer taking out gold. The prospect was exciting, and we appreciated Tony's generosity.

Kwanika and gold mining were put aside in our minds, however, for a later date. Things were still too new. We had much to do to get ready for our first winter at Manson Creek.

Then one day it all took a new turn.

"Keep it under your hats a while, folks. Jade has been discovered on Kwanika!" This excited comment came from our freighter, Bruce Russell, who lived and worked out of the Fort, but who also held placer claims on Kwanika and had just returned from spending a week there doing the annual assessment work.

"What did you say, Bruce? Jade? What does it mean? Is it good jade?" Larry had perked up immediately and was firing the questions faster than they could be answered. Seeing is believing, and Bruce produced from his pocket a four-inch drill core which they had extracted from one of the rocks.

"It's certainly green, Bruce. How did you guys stumble onto it?" In reply, Bruce told us the short happy story of the discovery:

"This Bart Reil, a businessman in Prince George (but a rockhound at heart), asked me about going up to my placer leases to do some looking around for jade because last year a boulder of the stuff was taken out from another creek not too far away. Bart has been interested in jade for years and has studied geological maps of the area. It was his opinion that the mineralogy of that country over west should be just right to be a jade-producing area.

"Well, we went to my camp and had no luck for a few days until this one morning when we were sitting on a big rock lacing up our boots. While we were talking, Bart was scratching idly at the rock until suddenly he became tremendously excited. The rock didn't scratch — typical of jade. We rushed to get the pack-sack drill and took out this core. Once we knew what we were looking for, we found jade rocks all up and down the creek and in the water, too. It's exciting and interesting, I tell you! Bart has gone to Germansen to get a plane back to Prince George. He's making some fast arrangements to get some of these bigger rocks out before the snow flies."

Not being babes in the woods, we realized that the only reason we were being let into the inner circle was that we, too, held claims on Kwanika, and next door to Bruce's. We agreed not to talk to others about it, but that didn't prevent a lot of thinking and talking among ourselves. Larry started scrounging through all the reference material we had, looking for information on this semi-precious gem material. With all the exciting hopes and possibilities whirling around in our heads, the limited bit of information in the encyclopedia was only frustrating.

It couldn't wait — we were all so eager and excited. Robert and Larry made hasty plans to get together a tent, sleeping bags, grub-box, camp stove, lantern, frying pan, and everything needed for a few days of prospecting.

When they returned three days later, their enthusiasm knew no bounds.

"We're rich! We've found it! What a wonderful new world! There's a beauty of a huge jade boulder on one of the claims, and all sorts of other jades in the creek. We even staked two more claims — one for you, Carolyn, and one for Maggie. That gives us two miles of the creek."

We absorbed the fellows' enthusiasm and began speculating on what it could mean to us and what we could do with the fortune which would be amassed. The big rock which commanded their attention was estimated in tonnage. At a low of $1.00 a pound the total value wouldn't be "just peanuts", but we were hoping for $10.00 per pound at least for the choice heart of the rock.

This brand new jade "thing" added another dimension to our already full and different life in the wilds of the B.C. interior. We were excited, but confused about what to do next. It was late in the year and already the first snows had fallen. We'd have to work fast, but were determined to attempt to get at least that one big rock out and initiate some money action. Some heavy equipment was required and fortunately, there was one man who hadn't left yet after his summer operation. He possessed just what we needed: a D-7 Caterpillar tractor. We invited him over, discreetly told him what we could of the whole happy story, and suggested a three-way partnership — his part being the "Cat" which would go into Kwanika, pull out the boulder, haul it on a stone-boat to where it could be trucked out. All expenses would be shared equally.

Harley Polan was our man, and he was nothing less than super-enthusiastic. No time was wasted. Harley went to work immediately getting his "Cat" welded up and ready to go. Camp equipment and grub were assembled and in just a few days the three partners were off. Three days later they had returned in the truck, and no sign of jade nor "Cat". The rock had been brought back to within twenty miles of Manson, but then the cat had broken down again and it seemed wisest to just leave things as they were for the winter. The rock would certainly be safe there, but our disappointment knew no bounds. We had flown too high and were suddenly grounded. Now we'd have to wait until next spring or summer. There were long faces in Manson Creek that day.

But we hadn't reckoned on Harley. His enthusiasm was something to behold. He went out, presumably for the winter, but got his needed parts and flew back into Germansen, prevailed on someone to drive him over to his Cat, repaired the machine, and came rolling through town to the delighted surprise of all of us. And there was the big rock — all our hopes and dreams — on its way out to make us a fortune. At the time it didn't occur to us that Harley was perhaps being too eager. We merely thought we had a terrific third partner.

After a round of conversation, a meal, and a short rest, Harley was on his way again to "walk" the Cat the 120 miles out to Fort St. James, and from there he would see that the boulder was trucked or railroaded to Vancouver to be processed.

Surprise! Two days later Mr. Polan was brought back to Manson Creek almost dead! He was only about thirty miles down the road when the Cat broke down again. The day before, he had lost his food supplies while taking the Cat through a creek instead of over the small bridge; the grub box had tipped and gone sailing irretrievably down the river. The temperature was hovering around zero (F) when Harley started walking back, cold, hungry and tired. He never would have made it without help.

His providential rescuers were "Wes" Westfall and Gene Jack. Gene had decided to take two of his trucks out for the winter since this unexpected Cat trip would have packed the foot or so of snow on the road sufficiently for driving a truck. It was a sudden and unplanned decision and was fortunate for Harley. We shuddered to think of the consequences, had Gene not made this move, because Harley told us that he was stopping to rest too often already, and eventually would have just gone to sleep by the side of the road and not awakened. I dare say he has thought about this narrow escape a few times.

Our third partner was dauntless. After a good warmup, a 24-hour rest, and plenty of food, he was ready to go again. He rode out with Gene and Wes who had decided to keep going, even though they would have to do their own plowing and shoveling where the road would be deep with snow. When they reached the Fort, Harley hired a truck with loading equipment and came back for the boulder. The Cat became a landmark by the side of the road because it sat there abandoned for three or four years. It was mortal after all!

Each monthly mail-day we eagerly anticipated word from Harley, and we sat in our isolation helplessly wondering what was going on. As month after month went by and not one single letter was received, we began to have doubts about our man. The only way we could revive our drooping spirits and keep hope rekindled was to remind ourselves that this jade rock was only the beginning and of course Harley also knew that it was only the beginning. He wouldn't jeopardize his partnership in such a beautiful set-up by doing anything ungentlemanly. At least he wouldn't so early in the operation. The time to start watching him more closely would be after we really got into jade-production in a big way.

But when spring rolled around and we still hadn't had a single word from Harley, we were furious. Larry took advantage of the first chance for a ride out, with the intention of looking up Mr. Third Partner. Harley wasn't hiding out and Larry found him easily. He told Larry that he had had the boulder cut and a couple of slices taken from it, and that it was now in storage in a friend's garage. He showed Larry a slice of some rather poor quality jade, claiming it was from our rock, and said he'd probably have trouble getting his freight, cutting, and storing expenses out of it. He was really crying the blues. There was no answer to why he hadn't kept in touch with us, and Larry just returned home in disgust. In the future he and Robert would go it alone. Harley had foolishly cut himself out of a promising future.

For centuries Oriental jade lovers have attributed mystical and almost psychical powers to this semi-precious rock. They claim that a relationship exists between jade and the human spirit, and they will strive for a lifetime to gain possession of even a small piece of this green good-luck stone.

We are certainly anything but superstitious, but the experience of Harley almost meeting his Maker in the snow-bound wilderness that winter was the first of a few cases of extreme bad luck and even actual disaster happening to a few people who in one way or another have attempted to cheat or deceive us in some way over jade.

Where There's Smoke . . . 12

When we city people switched over to a remote north woods type life, we found ourselves in a bygone era of gasoline lamps, wood stoves, and the ever-needed spark of ignition: the match. Civilization has come a long way since the day of the old-time kitchen matchbox, and indeed, cigarette lighters have almost banished the need for the handy pocket matches. The once-dreaded fear of a mother finding her small child playing with fire is almost a thing of the past now, and the occasional little rascal who is persistently intrigued with the power contained in a match-head is considered, by neighborhood mothers, to be something of a delinquent. Children in schools are given controlled demonstrations of the potential dangers of gasoline products, and especially of the gas and fire combinations.

One of the first things we discovered in our new pattern of living was the frequency of the need for matches, and the fact that a ready supply of them would become a household staple item. It was a few months before we cautiously permitted the girls to light-up the gas lamps, but that was no particular concern because even when we showed them how, they weren't eager to do it. But even with the awareness of danger constantly on our minds, and the resultant caution and care being practised, still that first winter had its moments of panic. In recollection, I wonder that we made it through the winter at all, since there were so many narrow escapes. We felt that some higher intelligence must be protecting us.

The little generator which supplied our night-time lighting system sat on a small sheltered platform at the back of the woodshed behind our house. The shed was stacked full with the winter wood supply, and was separated from the house by only a six-foot wide walkway. So one can imagine my horror in discovering, one October afternoon, the back of the woodshed ablaze! Standing nearby was little two-year-old Evy, his eyes wide with amazement, and his hand still clutching a long screwdriver with which he'd been "repairing" the motor. The generator hadn't been running, so he must have short-circuited something and the flying sparks feasted eagerly on gas-soaked surroundings.

"Evy!" I shrieked, grabbing him up and dashing to the back door to yell to anyone inside. "The generator and woodshed are on fire!!"

Larry, who had been resting on the couch, sprang into action and called for an old blanket as he raced by me and out the door. I snatched up the first available blanket and ran out with it. Larry was making frantic efforts at fire squelching, but called to us to start getting things out of the house. "It looks like everything's going up!"

Carolyn and the girls and I hurried back in, wondered where we should start, and went out again, foolishly, somehow not being able to believe that this hasty exit was going to be necessary. By that time our neighbor, Johnny, who had seen the smoke and heard the shouting, was on top of the wood stacks beating out the fire with another blanket, while Larry was dousing flames with water from an old rainbarrel. We onlookers just stood there watching breathlessly until it seemed that the men were getting the best of the situation.

The fire was conquered mainly because it hadn't really gotten a good start, because the men worked fast, and because of that old rain barrel which, only a few days before, someone had called "an eyesore." We had talked of a cleanup campaign to get rid of a few pieces of junk around the yard, but hadn't gotten to it as yet. The "eyesore" saved us.

I, personally, breathed my own prayer of thanks that Larry had returned home only about ten minutes before the terrible action started. Nothing — but nothing — could have persuaded *me* to go anywhere near that gas generator full of fire. Robert, who had been off in another direction with the other truck, arrived home a half-hour too late, thereby missing all the excitement. All he could see was the overhauling of a burned motor and a whole new re-wire job.

Well, we hadn't planned to have electricity anyway, and the generator being here was an unexpected bonus. So we went into winter with the gas lamps which *had* been planned for. It wasn't so bad, either. More like wilderness living. But about two months later, after having sent out for needed new parts, Robert had the generator running and there were lights in Manson Creek once again.

Another time we were enjoying a peaceful winter evening — 20-below outside, 70-above inside — when the sound of cracking glass behind the girls' bedroom door startled us. Cautiously we opened the door and peered into a room full of smoke. Either Lyn or Les had left a candle burning on the dresser top, and the overflowing wax had caught fire and smouldered right through the wood surface to the top layer of clothes in the drawer beneath. It was the big full-size mirror which we had heard cracking.

The three handy buckets of kitchen water were sufficient to squelch these small flames, as well as to douse Larry when he moved into the path of a bucketful which Leslee tossed at the right moment (or was it the wrong moment?). Anyway, the rest of us declared Les the heroine of the day, while Larry went grumbling off to change clothes. I was glad we could still laugh in times of tension.

There aren't too many people with wood stoves who start the fire with shavings anymore. Usually some type of quick-starter is used, be it kerosene, diesel, oil-soaked paper, used car-oil, or whatever. Our method was a squirt-bottle of kerosene. To keep this plastic bottle supplied, there was a large can of kerosene on the back porch. Just next to it was a can of naphtha gas used for filling Coleman stoves and lamps. Only a few times did the contents of the two cans get mistakenly switched. The highly volatile naphtha explodes with a not-soon-to-be-forgotten suddenness when a match is applied. Damage would be confined to shattered nerves and singed eyebrows. The only reason the explosions weren't worse was that not much fuel is squirted on the wood in the first place.

On another occasion Larry had gone into the store to add a log to the fire, and discovered the place full of smoke. Someone had put a log too near the outside of the barrel-stove. It must have been smouldering there for several hours. This particular day was another cold wintry one, so our problem proved to be how to get the smoke out of the store without letting too much arctic weather in through the open door. All we could decide was to build up the fire in the heater and just leave the door open for as short a time as would be necessary. There was no loss here, and no damage to any of the goods, but again the nerve-shattering thoughts of what might have been if . . .

The first day we moved into Hamiltons' house, things were so busy and hectic that we brought in the Coleman stove for quick lunches and frequent pots of coffee. Somehow that little stove proved so handy, when we didn't want to fire up the wood stove, that it remained forever a vital part of our kitchen. When the first one wore out, it was replaced with another. Only a few times did these camp stoves act erratically enough to start small fires, and in each case it was not the fault of the stove. These were merely baking-soda extinguishable fires — nothing more serious — but provided their own moments of panic and excitement.

And only once did the squirt-bottle of kerosene get knocked down onto a hot stove — with startling results.

Of course it's terribly risky to have numerous gasoline products around within easy access of children, to say nothing of ourselves. All one has to do, while filling or lighting a gas lamp or stove, is be momentarily distracted or be thinking of something other than what he is doing, and a careless action *could* mean disaster. The nearest Fire Department is 120 miles away.

Since we do sell and use these products, and since we must keep them in ready availability, we have had several different lessons with the children in proper handling. Larry would deliberately spill a little gas on bare ground and apply a match. If the sudden jumps of the onlookers were any indication, the lessons were correctly learned.

Fire is an awesome necessity. It has a voracious appetite which is never appeased. It can be used to save a life with exactly the same eagerness that it will take a life. Try to use this most fearsome tool with recklessness and it will strike back with vengeance. Used with due respect for its potential, great and mighty things can be achieved.

Even though we thought we were using undue caution and care, the balance was tipsy that first winter. Certainly fire was our friend, but was it a two-faced friend?

Our First Northern Winter

Winter months this far north on the globe are November through April or May, and during this time the snow conditions on the road cut us off from the rest of the world. In later years the road would be plowed open early in spring, but the first year Manson Creek was a tight little island to itself except for the arrival of the mail plane each month.

How we can bear to live so remotely, and what on earth we find to do for seven months in this lonely, far away spot, are questions which perplex the summer tourists. The idea of isolation terrifies some people. Others panic at the thought of no professional medical assistance in case of emergencies. Many are concerned with how people make a living here and how the children get their schooling. The B.C. Government Correspondence School is considered by all those who know little or nothing about it, to be the ideal educational method. Interestingly enough, however, that is the only 'fly in the ointment' in the whole scene. Our attitude about education comprises a big part of our philosophy of life; and not knowing what we were going into, we still felt unafraid in giving up that large segment of the average child's routine. Correspondence lessons were utilized but we consider them far from the ideal educational medium.

To us, winter living could be summed up in one word: PEACEFUL. Work, play, sleep, reading — everything is entirely at one's own pace. Each day is started without alarm clocks, without having to rush to work or to school after gulping down a hurried breakfast or no breakfast at all. Life here could be likened to every man's dream of the desert island he'd love to retire to, providing his taste runs to the colder climate.

We had lived the nine-to-five workday routine just as all our contemporaries were doing, except that Larry's hours had been more like seven-to-eleven due to all the meetings and extra-curricular

55

obligations of the school principal's position. Having left all that behind, the new joy and contentment derived from this relaxed approach to each day was almost indescribable. Many were the mornings when we'd stand around the fire with that first cup of coffee and deplore the plight of all our friends and relatives back home who were well into their day's work already after having suffered the daily recurring torture of the morning rush routine to get there on time.

The world would be in sad shape if everyone suddenly revolted as we did. Fortunately no fear of that, however. This freedom we love would not be contentment to many who find security and peace-of-mind in accustomed regularity. Nonetheless, a very large percentage of family men are terribly dissatisfied with their monotonous routines, feel trapped, and would love to get away to something like this. We have talked to them over the years. They are either too bogged down with bills, or their wives just couldn't take it, or their children wouldn't want to leave their friends, or some other stumbling block is too great for them. Admittedly, it does take cooperation from the family and a certain amount of determination and just plain guts. We selfishly gloat over the fact that everyone who expresses the desire to live as we do just can't seem to find it possible to do so.

*   *   *   *   *   *

Basic survival anywhere is a matter of having sufficient food and keeping warm. There were no worries about food, but keeping warm was a never-ending effort. We had been used to automatic heating for too long and were forever forgetting to add wood to the fire. The house would be pleasantly warm and everyone busily occupied, when suddenly someone would groan that it was getting cold. Sure enough, a look inside the heater would find the fire down to embers and we'd have to start it going again. Lyn and Les were the kindling choppers but they seldom had enough of this fine-cut wood in reserve. One of the colder nights when the box was empty, the kids got the brilliant idea of rolling a chopping block into the house. I sputtered protests at first — one just doesn't chop wood in the house! But in the next breath, after stepping outside and right back in again because the night was so bitterly cold, I relented. We had a consultation and decided that if the kids picked times when no one was trying to sleep or concentrate on some project, they might cut kindling in the house during the worst of winter. This chopping block became a friend. When it was not being utilized for its designated purpose, it became a spare seat by the stove. We named it "Chip-n-chop," immortalizing it as a distant relative to an elegant line of furniture. It held its honoured spot as a fireside seat for a few years

56

until, on a redecorating splurge, we all reluctantly agreed that our friend must go.

Household routines all take longer to accomplish without the time and labour saving conveniences which are so much a part of the city home. Cooking with a wood stove requires building up the fire to the desired temperature instead of setting a thermostat. No supermarkets nearby means that all bread for the family must be home baked, as well as all the cakes, cookies, buns, pies, and other goodies. Although meat is usually plentiful, it must be cut, trimmed and processed before using. Fresh milk is not available by the quart or half-gallon; it comes in dry form and must be mixed a few hours before using. No quick-cooking meals or T.V. dinners are available in our little Trading Post.

In the laundry room no automatic washer makes for an all-day job on washday. No hot-water taps means that all water which needs to be hot for its purpose must be heated on the stove. Indeed, no running water at all means that all water for any purpose must be hauled in by bucket. It didn't take us long to latch onto the advantage of catching all the summer rainwater we could keep contained; and in winter lovely bath and wash water is obtained by melting chunks of ice and snow. All these little tricks save endless trips to the creek.

Lack of refrigeration makes food storage a problem in the summer-time. Too much cold in winter also creates other worries: which foods to let freeze, which ones to just keep cold, and where to keep them cold without freezing. Toasters, waffle irons, mixers, and other handy everyday appliances which depend on electricity have no place in the wilderness kitchen.

Motors are often a problem in the worst of winter. If one plans to use a chainsaw or the washing machine, for instance, it's a good idea to have them inside by the fire overnight. Later on, when we bought a generator, it was necessary to house it in a building large enough to also accommodate a small wood stove. The stove would be fired-up for a few hours each day before generator turning-on time, in order to soften up the congealed oil.

Trucks, too, are difficult to start in sub-zero weather without applying some form of heat to the oil pan underneath. In the bush there are various ways to accomplish this, even to the cautious use of a blow torch. But in northern cities where working people have to depend on cars and trucks for transportation, a very common sight is the cord running from an electrical source to the block heater on the vehicle parked outside. This keeps the car motor warm for ease in starting the next morning. I had never seen this before coming to Canada.

And then there is the incomparable experience of the trip to the outhouse at thirty-below! Since we survived a decade of this type of roughing it, and since no one ever suffered ill effects from this type of exposure, all one can assume is that the human body is tougher than most people suppose. We felt that the advantages of our bush life outweighed by far the few disadvantages. At any rate, the facility is not called "the library" because no one spends any extra time browsing there. The use of a bedroom chamber pot at night is neither common nor uncommon. Each family decides for itself, and after all it really is a small matter and a personal one.

In the beginning the man of the family may have a heavy work load if he has to clear ground for a cabin, cut logs, build the home, cut and haul in firewood, build furniture, plow the ground if there is to be a garden, kill and butcher the meat supply. But with most of these jobs, when they are done, they are done. They are not everyday routine time-consuming operations, and after things are set up the man is more or less free. On the other hand, his woman, being newly transported into this rural life style, finds all her daily work takes more time to accomplish. This being so, it is not uncommon to see the traditional male and female roles overlapping or even being occasionally switched. Dad might be found washing the dishes, kneading bread, or even preparing a meal, while mother could be outside doing some wood-chopping, gardening, or water-bucket filling. The sensible, unwritten rule of wilderness living is that each person know how to do everything involved with daily subsistence.

Actually, if the home is a happy one and the woman has accompanied her man willingly into this type of life, then each chore attempted by each member of the family is approached with an attitude of contributing to the family comfort and pleasure. Total family togetherness, and cooperative, contented, unrebellious children are the satisfying rewards.

But there is one chore which is neither typically the man's nor the woman's, and each family is obliged to work out its own compromises: WHO IS GOING TO CRAWL OUT OF A WARM BED ON A COLD MORNING TO GET THE WOOD FIRE STARTED? It's almost physical pain to even think about voluntarily emerging from blessed warmth to the chill of a cold kitchen when it's twenty-below outside. By the second winter we had worked out a satisfactory solution to this horrible task. We staggered sleeping hours and kept the fires going all night. This might seem far from ideal but it worked out well for us and gradually evolved from our living habits. Lyn and Les had discovered by then that schoolwork was more easily accomplished in the evening when there were fewer distractions. Their staying-up hours became later and later, even until four or five in the morning; but still there were advantages which satisfied everyone. A small house with five people together for the total waking hours seven days a week can become less than ideal in the best of circumstances. So in the late quiet hours the girls would do their studying, write letters, wash and set their hair, and indulge in the inevitable girl-talk which is a trademark of teen-age. Before going to bed they'd fill the stove with logs and close the vents for slower burning. Then one would make a quick trip over to the store to throw some logs in that fire, too. By 9:00 when Larry and I got up, the house would still be pleasantly warm, and the goods in the store would have survived another night with no fear of freezing. There was a bonus in it for us, too. Larry and I had a few quiet hours of our own in the morning to drink coffee and read, write letters, or just talk things over. We became very jealous of this particular period of time and would grumble inwardly on the rare occasion when it might be interrupted by a visitor.

The girls would be incommunicado until the afternoon hours, of course, but we all thrived nicely with the arrangement for a few months in the dead of winter. When the days began lengthening out and warming up, then the girls began evening-out the sleep time to more normal hours.

Evy had his own little homemade bunk in our room. He would go to bed when we did unless he'd already fallen asleep on the couch. He'd usually sleep a little later in the morning, but when he'd finally appear, ready for another day, Larry and I were forced into the inevitable. Our early morning solitude was over. Toddlers just don't think much of peace and quiet.

Some hardy souls might roar indignantly at me calling 9:00 a.m. "early morning hours." A few of the oldtimers around feel the need for regularity and are up at 6:30 summer or winter. But they will have to admit that from the middle of November through until the end of January it's still too dark inside the house even at 8:00 in the morning to maneuver without a lamp turned on. And regardless of the oldtiners and their habits, we found that it suited our convenience to begin the day at the hour we chose to wake up. Breakfast would always be late — around noon, dinner about five, and invariably a light lunch at midnight. It was fun to jumble up traditional eating and sleeping hours. We did everything exactly the way we felt like doing.

Except on bitterly cold days we were in and out of the house a great deal. When brilliant sunshine on the heavy blanket of snow makes sunglasses a necessity, and when the expanse of sky is a sharp crystal blue, life and health seem a prized possession. Invariably, someone admiring the day will comment that if the folks back home could be suddenly transported here, they would probably pass out from fresh air inhalation. But in the next breath we'd be deploring the dreadful truth that in Southern California, as in any densely populated metropolis over the United States, there are children and young people who have never in their lives seen a day as sparklingly clear as any of our unclouded days. The worst pollution we can come up with is the rolling, fragrant smoke from cabin stovepipes.

We might as well have declared a week-long holiday in the middle of each month, in honour of the mail coming in. Beginning about the tenth of the month we start frantically writing and answering letters, and by the fourteenth each of the residents, usually at separate intervals, starts dropping in to speculate on the possibility of the mail plane coming in on time. Without fail, everyone is in evidence on the fifteenth, regardless of weather conditions. If the sky looks darkly threatening, we commiserate but still hope. If flying is absolutely impossible and the day shows no sign of clearing, the folks disperse to their own homes and return the next day full of renewed hope.

When the longed-for aircraft finally does circle town and heads for the lake three miles away, Larry and Robert and anyone else who so desires, takes off on snowshoes, carrying back-packs and pulling sleds. Sometimes Jack and Winnie go along with their dog-sled and this makes the hauling of mail sacks considerably easier.

At the same time the incoming mail is received, our outgoing sack of letters is handed over to the pilot. This being the case, bills to be paid and questions to be answered have to wait another month for the next plane. A running correspondance with a friend is difficult and might falter with the long delays at our end of the line. But our consolation is in the fact that mail once a month is better than no mail at all, which might have been our fate had we carried out our original intention of going off completely by ourselves to build our homes by a lake.

November and May are headache months for the mail. The ice on the lakes is either in process of forming or breaking up, and either way the planes cannot land. The mail always gets in somehow — by truck, tractor, or helicopter — but the confusion is in not knowing when to expect it. It might be an additional two weeks late, but it gets in. I can remember only once when an entire month was skipped.

Actual winter climate was the biggest surprise for all of us. We had thought the temperature would drop to well below zero and stay there for four or five months. We had expected blizzards and snow piled so high we'd have to tunnel out the front door after a storm. I remember even suggesting to Bob and Carolyn that perhaps we should rig up a communication line of some sort in case we couldn't leave our respective homes for a few days at a time.

The first winter we started the habit of setting a gas drum out in the flat area so we could watch the snow level climb. The drum is thirty-six inches tall and almost never have we seen snow piled higher. Of course much more than that falls, but it melts a little and packs down some before the next snow adds its inches. As for tunneling out the door, we haven't had to do much more than sweep a layer of newly blown snow off the porch.

Winter temperatures probably average around zero F., and with the approach of spring the average rises to fifteen or twenty above. The mercury will drop to forty or fifty below a few times each year, but a common winter low point is twenty below. All during this season there are drastic ups and downs to the thermometer, just as there are anywhere, but our variations are on a lower range. On the coldest days we usually stay indoors talking or reading with the pleasant aroma of home baking in the background. Temperatures in the fifteen-below to fifteen-above range are conducive to snowshoe walking, wood chopping, or any of the outdoor activities which keep one moving about. But when the mercury registers twenty-above or warmer, everyone starts shedding coats, caps, and mittens. It's shirtsleeves weather in the North and we all revel in it.

A phenomenon which warm-climate residents will find hard to believe is that although we shiver at the freezing point in the fall when temperatures are heading downward, after we've experienced some real winter weather, any rise in the mercury to twenty-above is considered a spring day. This must appear ridiculous, I know, but each person who has come north to live has wonderingly experienced this same reaction over and over again.

Christmas . . . and No Gifts 14

According to the calendar the end of the year was upon us but no one was making out Christmas lists or doing much of any thinking about holiday plans. Nor were there any commercial forces at work to influence us. In Manson Creek there were no gaily decorated streets and stores, no bustling shoppers, no twice or thrice a day bundles of Christmas mail being delivered, not even any Christmas music since our battery-powered radio had failed us. The mail plane due to arrive December fifteenth would be too early to catch the big bulk of incoming seasonal cards and letter from our friends back home.

All these stark facts were not bothering anyone — in fact it was here that we suddenly realized a lot about what Christmas has come to mean to most people. Earlier and earlier each year the world of commercialism begins its massive brainwash program. Every business-house looks for an upswing in sales and profits during the holiday season. And what's frightening is that each year must be bigger and better than the previous one or something is terribly wrong with their advertising program! We felt fortunate to be out from under this pressure. Now we could take an entirely different approach — and did. But the "approach" was not planned. We just let things take their natural course as the days of December came and went. Life continued in its uncomplicated and unhurried manner.

By mid-December Carolyn and I got out the cookbooks and our hoarded inventory of special holiday ingredients, and began what turned into a three-day baking spree. We made fruit-cakes, several kinds of cookies, a huge pan of fudge, and experimented with several other candy recipes. Knowing that the old-timers of the area would probably have nothing in the way of any festivities, we decided between us to do up a small box of our baked goodies for each of them. (This became a tradition which we continued each year as long as we lived at

Manson.)

It wasn't until the twenty-third that Lyn glanced at the calendar and announced with no little urgency, "Hey, we've got to get a Christmas tree. It's almost Christmas!"

I had thought the house far too small to introduce another sizeable object, but Lyn pointed out that a little tree could sit on one end of the long desk. To my next observation that we hadn't brought any tree-trimmings, the girls responded that we could make things to hang from the branches.

I was outnumbered, so off they went on showshoes, brandishing an axe. Living right in the area where Christmas trees are born and raised, the only problem one has in making a selection is just in the choosing of one from the limitless array of possibilities. But within an hour the girls were back with a perfectly formed, bushy, three-foot-tall spruce which was exactly right for its designated spot.

That evening we all went to work with aluminum foil, coloured paper, paste, scissors, and as a finishing touch, long popcorn strands were looped over the branches. I won't say that the finished product was the loveliest Christmas tree we'd ever decorated, but this one had a charm all its own and provided the spark which set off the festive spirit among us.

Everyone understood that there would be no gifts under the tree this year. Being involved in so much newness in lifestyle, we hadn't thought about ordering anything by mail until too late, and lacking foresight, neither had we tucked away any gifty things when packing the trucks for the trip, back in California. The gift-part of Christmas seemed unimportant. Even the girls were taking a more adult view of this custom which has gotten so completely out of hand. I had thought it was only Carolyn and I who had just a tiny bit of nostalgia for the family-type celebrations of the past which we were used to, and only because we both came from large families. But on Christmas Eve after the kids had gone to bed, Larry asked if there wasn't some little something we could surprise them with next morning. Well, I knew we had nothing stashed away around the house, so we went over to the Trading Post to have a look around. All we could come up with was some chocolate bars, gum and a dollar bill for each. We wrapped the little items separately, labelled them, and hung them around the tree. Next morning the reaction was heart-warming. Not expecting anything, the girls' surprise and pleasure at our little gesture was mature beyond their years. These were the same ones who, on Christmas mornings of the past, would scrounge around the base and branches of the tree to be sure that nothing had been missed; the same two who used to do what all their friends did — compare numbers and types of gifts. I can't truthfully say that we were finding the real meaning of Christmas, because there wasn't any particular religious emphasis, either. But what we did seem to be accomplishing was a more rational and satisfactory approach to this holiday.

As far as Christmas dinner was concerned, we were completely tradition-bound. Who could improve on the exquisite all-day cooking fragrance of a roasting turkey with its accompanying dressing, gravy, mashed potatoes, cranberry, gelatin salad, hot biscuits, and topped off with the pie which no one ever has room for?

But for me, personally, the high point of the season occurred when Johnny brought over his portable radio (knowing that ours was out of commission) and urged us to keep it a few days to listen to some Christmas music. Suddenly I realized how music-starved I'd been. For two days I was hardly out of earshot of that radio. Music had been a big part of my life for as long as I could remember. My mother had been our church organist, and I had played piano and flute in orchestras all during school years. The extent of my music appreciation broadened expansively after meeting Larry. He and I used to go to the "Symphonies Under the Stars" at Hollywood Bowl several times each summer, and Larry possessed an enviable collection of records. In this way my taste in music had developed to include classical and popular, sacred and secular, vocal and instrumental. So with the loan of Johnny's radio, our house was filled for two days with the delightful sounds of all the lovely songs, carols, and folk-music of the season. The rest of the family may have taken a more matter-of-fact approach to the temporary visitor in our home, but for me, personally, the feast of musical sounds of Christmas was sumptious. Our neighbor's generous gesture meant more to me than he could possibly have realized.

* * * * * *

On New Year's Eve we were feeling quietly festive in honour of the first half-year of our Canadian adventure-in-living. Outside, the raging elements were at war with one-another. Wind whistled around the corners of buildings, and fat snowflakes whizzed by the windows at the horizontal rather than vertical angle. Actual temperature was only fifteen degrees F., but the whipping wind forced a chill-factor to the air of well below zero.

Inside the house, however, all was calm with the wood fire crackling merrily and warmth pervading the room. Chairs were drawn up and the family, together with our young partners who by now were more like family members, were in a mood of recollection. Two-year-old Everett had fallen asleep on the couch, but our daughters were certainly going to stay up and awake until that magic moment on the clock. It didn't matter that the New Year would commence with no tooting horns or balloons or confetti at Manson Creek. In fact, since our radio had refused to perform, we weren't even sure about the correctness of our clock. We might miss midnight by a few minutes or even start observing the New Year five minutes too soon.

"Well, everyone," said I, breaking into the temporary quiet reverie, "when we were planning this change in our life style back there in California, would you have ever guessed it could have turned out so great?" This comment of mine seemed to trigger thoughts and responses.

Leslee replied at once, "The most exciting thing I remember is the night we got stuck in the snowbank. Wouldn't Grandma and Grandpa have had kittens if they had known what we were doing!" It had happened only a few weeks previously when the foot-or-so of early winter snow had been packed by Harley Polan's D-7 Cat trip through town. We had decided to take advantage of the situation and visit our new friends at Germansen Landing (twenty miles away) before the road closed up completely for the winter. All went well until seven miles from our destination where a rear-wheel slid off the edge of the road. In attempting to get back on, the wheel spun and sank hopelessly down the slight bank. There we were — helpless! Larry volunteered to walk the seven miles to Germansen for assistance, so while he was gone the rest of us crowded into the two large zipped-together sleeping bags and lay there in the open back of the truck looking up at the magnificent star-studded sky. Later on, Robert built a bonfire in the road using short, dry twigs, a little gasoline, and then an armload of larger branches. In moments the fire was roaring. A basic rule of *always* carrying emergency rations when traveling in the bush had not been forgotten. We dug into the apples and chocolate bars with gusto, considering it more of a picnic than a crisis. Within a few hours Larry returned with a Jeep and winched out the truck. But many times during the wait we had commented that the folks home in California would be horrified had they known that while they were sitting comfortably in their living rooms watching television, we were stranded many miles from nowhere in zero weather.

"You know something? My head still hurts from Lyn's accidently knocking the kindling-chopping axe off the top shelf onto my skull. Have you all thought how the course of your lives might have suddenly changed if the sharp side of the axe had hit?" Larry had, indeed, both escaped serious injury and also suffered a good-sized knot on his head as a result of this scary accident that had happened a few days previously. It was a sobering thought for a moment.

Then Robert volunteered that it had been maddening to have the radio out of commission on the day President Kennedy had been shot. "Remember how we scrounged through everything to find something to get that damn radio working so we could hear what was going on?"

Memories of that November 22nd day in infamy were fresh in our minds again. Johnny had picked up the tragic event in Dallas on his radio, and we, in desperation at our lack of communications, had spent most of the day back and forth to his cabin to listen to the progression of sad events. That day we brand-new Canadian "landed immigrants" had been more than a little aware of the pulse of American blood in our veins.

All was quiet around the fireplace for a bit and someone got up to refill coffee mugs. Logs in the fire continued with their mood-inspiring snapping and crackling.

Then Carolyn spoke up: "I don't know if we'll ever get used to this once-a-month mail delivery. I guess its better than none at all, though." The post office was an integral part of the town, and Robert's wife had been selected to oversee its operations as Postmistress. The mail service did seem terribly infrequent, but we kept reminding ourselves that had we carried out our original intentions we might have had no mail deliveries at all.

Lynlee, our older daughter, voiced a few loud complaints about the amount of schoolwork required by correspondence school's Grade 8, as compared to what she had been used to in public school back home.

It was nearing midnight and the girls were trying to think up some ingenious excitement for the occasion. They put their heads together and came up with the idea of making popcorn.

"You folks just sit still now. We'll take care of everything," they announced bouncing up. The little Coleman stove was brought out into the room, fired up, and the covered pan of popping corn set on the burner. Just as the internal action was getting into full force, Lyn reached over and removed the lid. Popcorn burst out into the air and rolled all over the room. It was a hilarious few moments and a fitting climax to our first year-end in the Canadian bush.

Neighbourly Contributions 15

That first winter the total Manson Creek population consisted of Jack and Winnie Thomson (trappers), Johnny Neilsen, Pete Langley, and Bob Watson (all retired prospectors and living alone), Robert and Carolyn, and the five of us Owens. It is unlikely that this small group of people would have sought out each other's company in a social way anywhere except in an isolated spot such as this. But the thing we had in common was the fact that each of us did at some time make the decision for this remote way of life, and that fact alone was a starting point. We found it advantageous to have a few others living nearby to be able to call on for advice at times. Everyone who has lived has had experiences, and we needed more than once to tap the experienced wisdom of our northern neighbors in this unfamiliar living situation.

In and around Manson and Germansen about four trapping areas converge. Jack and Winnie Thomson (unlike the other trappers who only come in for the season) are year-round residents. They live six miles up the Manson, and spend most of each winter tending the lines inside their own 150-square-mile area.

Larry and I have a philosophy about what we consider needless bloodshed, and it extends most definitely to the trapping of animals for fur. Regardless of our personal opinions, however, trapping goes on and will continue to go on until either the vain females (human) change their status symbol, or the synthetic fur industry perfects itself. I predict the latter, if either, to happen first.

Jack has been a prospector and fur-trapper ever since coming to Canada from England during the "hungry thirties." He fought with the Canadian forces in Europe during World War II, was wounded, discharged, and returned home to Manson Creek. The quiet, unobtrusive, industrious nature of this man left his friends completely dumbfounded when he unexpectedly married one of the boisterous Fort

St. James Indian girls nineteen years his junior. Heads were shaking in disbelief and dismay, and everyone wondered what had gotten into Jack. But Winnie was a fine wife for Jack and the head-waggers eventually were eating their words. She is an immaculate housekeeper whose worst habit is burning wood in excessive amounts. Together they have proved the theory held by many that an intermingling of races is conducive to fine-looking offspring. The proof is there to see in their son.

But for a few years before Peter was born, Winnie was a constant companion with Jack, snowshoeing along the trails of his territory to set traps, and then back a few days later to, hopefully, pick up the animals. They had three small cabins conveniently located along the way and stocked with food and firewood for overnight stops.

Trapping is not an easy occupation, and has its share of headaches and worry. Snaring the animal is only the beginning. After a deft, careful skinning, the pelts are hung up to dry. Beaver are opened up and stretched to a perfect circle on a round rack. The furry hide of squirrel, mink, weasel (ermine), lynx, and others are peeled off the animal and dried inside-out like a sausage casing.

A bundle of pelts will be packaged, insured, and mailed to an established fur buyer. From that point on, the trapper is at the mercy of the buyer. A measure of confidence is gained by dealing with the same buyer over a period of time, and the trapper will have a sketchy idea of the price his furs will bring because the "going market price" is published and mailed out monthly. But the difference between hoped-for and actual money received is not entirely determined by fluctuations in the market. To be taken into consideration are flaws in the pelts, imperfections in the skinning job, over-size or undersize skins, and the season in which the fur is taken. It would be a fair guess to say that the integrity of the buyer also enters the picture.

Winnie has retained the fast-diminishing art of Indian beadwork and leathercraft. She tans moosehide and makes mukluks, moccasins, gloves, jackets, belts, and gun cases. Her work has been one of the tourist attractions of our store.

*   *   *   *   *   *

At eighty-two years of age, Bob Watson, Canadian war veteran and retired member of the Royal Canadian Mounted Police, was the old-timer of Manson Creek. (He has since died.) He was lean and strong, and an active courtly-type gentleman. He would spend the beautiful days of summer tramping around the hills prospecting for anything of a mineral nature which might represent a new "find" and thereby make his fortune. Bob never discovered anything great, but he was part of the group who found the first jade boulder in this part of the country a year before we arrived in Canada.

During the winter months Bob would cut firewood. He must have kept a five years' supply ahead at all times. Getting the wood from where it was cut down to his cabin had been a problem until Bob designed and built a chute which guided the logs, by gravity, from the hillside behind his home right down to the side of his cabin. He was a "loner" and liked to solve his own problems. He had no vehicles; all traveling was on foot or by snowshoe. His cabin was six miles upstream on the Manson, and this fact alone necessitated a fair bit of hiking just to come to town for mail and supplies.

"Wes" Westfall has often related the story of the first time he met Mr. Watson in the store at Germansen Landing. Bob had purchased a goodly supply of grub — about forty or fifty pounds worth — and had it all conveniently loaded into his packsack. Wes figured he'd lend a hand so he reached over to lift up the pack and faltered with the unexpected weight. Bob laughed, effortlessly picked it up, put his arms through the straps, and took off at a brisk pace to accomplish the ten-mile trip back home before dark.

Larry and I both tend to feel impatient with the hard-of-hearing, although we try not to let it show. It's incredible to us that people will readily accept the assistance of eye-glasses and dentures, but ignore or even deny needing a hearing aid.

I suppose that those guilty of this attitude are unaware of the fact that people are shouting at them. Bob and several others in our small town fall into this category, unfortunately.

One day in the store Bob asked for a pound of butter.

"Butter or margarine?" I questioned.

"Butter, please," Bob replied.

"It's better with butter!" I flippantly commented as I reached for the item.

"I beg your pardon?"

Me again, louder: "It's better with butter."

Bob: "I'm sorry, I still didn't get that."

"It's just a slogan the butter producers use," I said loudly and clearly, but I was tired of the little game. Many facetious comments lose all their charm in repetition. Once more I said slowly and precisely, "It's better with butter."

Bob smiled and nodded affirmatively, "Yes, I *do* like butter."

Me: (sigh).

But one day Bob returned from a trip out to the city and proudly showed us the new hearing aid which he had finally been convinced, by someone, that he needed. We took him over to the house so he could tell us about his most recent adventures. Bob put the device to his ear and left it there during the conversation, all the while assuring us that he really had needed this new-fangled attachment. Suddenly he cocked his head, listened intently, and looked at us with the most curious expression. He had been watching Evy who was unconcernedly turning the pages of a magazine at the other end of the table.

"That's the first time in years I can remember hearing the sound of pages being turned," he remarked. We considered that a fantastic tribute to the hearing aid industry.

But poor old Bob had lived alone too long with no one to talk to but himself. Not needing the hearing device at home, he set it up on a shelf and proceeded to forget all about it.

Whenever he'd come to town, we'd greet him with, "How's the new gadget, Bob?"

"I beg your pardon?"

*   *   *   *   *   *

If anyone around town ever deserved the title, "Mayor of Manson Creek," it would be Johnny Neilsen. His cabin is about a hundred yards up the road from us and during the entire time the road is open, almost as many cars drive up and stop at Johnny's as will come to the store or to our house. He has many friends who've known him for years, and many of the passers-through have only heard about Johnny but want to meet him. Overnight accommodation is available in the back room of his cabin and he has put up and breakfasted many a passing prospector, mining engineer, traveling R.C.M.P. officer, or hunting enthusiast.

Johnny has been and still is the generally acknowledged, uncrowned, and sometimes disputed cribbage champion of these parts. His "crib" board is almost famous, and seldom does a day go by or car stop at the door but that a game is inevitably underway. The wall of his cabin is decorated with trophies and plaques attesting to Mr. John Neilsen's championship cribbage playing. The fact that these awards were made up by pranksters is strictly incidental.

The many gestures of helpfulness by our closest neighbor were evident especially during the first few years of our getting acclimated and accustomed to this new life. Evy struck a responsive note in Johnny's grandfatherly instincts right at the beginning. John became the boot-mender, the toy fixer, the dispenser of leftover pancakes, and the best all-around buddy a youngster could wish for. The friendship thrived beautifully during the winter months. Evy has been known to take an early morning stroll up the road, pajama-clad and barefoot in the snow, in order to casually request Johnny to scratch his back.

Summertime, however, was another matter. Evy would see less and less of his friend because there were just too many strangers around the "other house" for his bashful nature to cope with. Unperturbed, Evy didn't seem to consider it a great loss. He had much digging in the dirt, mud-pie making, and general exploring to while away the long summer days.

John came from Denmark and speaks with a decided Scandinavian accent. As a young man he traveled and worked on a tramp steamer for a number of years, signed off at Canada, and made his way to the interior of British Columbia to try his luck at gold mining. He has lived and worked in most all of the areas up here, but after settling in Manson Creek he declared flatly that there just isn't any other place to live! Johnny has staked placer claims, worked the claims for gold, sold the claims, restaked elsewhere and gone the same route many times. Now he is retired and enjoys his simple, leisurely life. The first year of our acquaintance, Johnny was as vain as a woman about his age. All he would say was that he was a long ways from being pensioned off. He lives alone in his spotlessly clean cabin. Johnny's housekeeping would put most women's to shame.

*　　*　　*　　*　　*　　*

Pete Langley was a daily visitor at Johnny's, but although we'd see Pete walking across the road or working at his wood pile, we didn't get to know him very well until the second year. His appearance was for all the world that of a fictional sea captain — tall, massive of build, about sixty years of age, a full head of white crew-cut hair, and even a decided limp caused by a stiff knee joint which we romantically and mistakenly thought at first was a wooden leg.

Pete had a little one-man placer operation down on the creek, and Larry and Robert used to help him occasionally shovel dirt into the sluice box. The fellows talked with Pete as they worked, and thus got to know him much sooner than the rest of us. Whenever he had to come to the store, he'd bring Johnny along for moral support, knowing that he'd find either me or one of the girls behind the counter. Poor bashful Pete couldn't manage much more than a weak "Hello" and would set about the hurried selection of his purchases. I had the distinct feeling that he resented so many women and children suddenly appearing on the scene in this traditionally "man's country".

It wasn't until one New Year's Eve that we found out differently. Johnny and Pete had planned a noisy surprise for midnight when all the few residents were gathered together for a small observance of the occasion. No one paid any particular attention when Pete stepped outside a few minutes before twelve. The radio was playing and as the special moment was upon us, we all toasted the New Year! But Johnny had a concerned look on his face and slipped outside. In just a few moments he was back, and with him an ashen Pete who was clutching his bloody, mangled right hand. The dynamite cap had exploded, but not in the intended place!

Pete, the experienced powder man, was more chagrined over his miserable failure than he was concerned about his hand. He did his best to make light of the drasitc situation and was ashamed of himself for having spoiled the party. All his apologies and regrets went unnoticed as Larry sprang into action and Robert dashed for the door. Larry called for lots of water and the first aid kit, while Robert frantically ran back to our home to attempt to get a phone call out for help. (A radio-telephone had been obtained as an absolute necessity for going into the second winter of isolation.) Transmission and reception at night, however, was almost never possible. We were all in a panic: here was our first emergency, and we couldn't summon help!

Meanwhile, back at the scene of action, Larry had cleaned and temporarily bandaged the mangled fingers. In whispered consultation the men decided that the most humane thing to do for Pete would be to get him blind drunk. At least the hours would pass more rapidly and the pain would be minimal while he was unconscious. So the party carried on with real purpose and intent. But as the hours wore on, instead of passing out, Pete became more talkative. He used his bloody, bandaged hand for gesturing and back-slapping, and kept telling us all again and again what wonderful people we were. By morning he was still awake, feeling no pain, and didn't seem much worse for the wear. When we finally got the call through and help arrived, the wound was twenty-four hours old.

Pete returned the next spring minus one finger and part of another. But the change in his personality was fantastic. He greeted us all like long-lost friends. No more signs of bashfulness with us were ever evident again. But we'd chuckle to ourselves when a stranger would attempt to engage Pete in conversation. He was still shy with new acquaintances, and that made his change in attitude toward us even more heart-warming.

School by Correspondence 16

Since Larry had been involved with Public Schools for twelve years, it was natural that we gave much thought to the education of our children as we were planning this northern adventure. We felt that even if formal education in actual schoolrooms might turn out to be non-existent (which it undoubtedly would) still the bush-life experience would be richly rewarding in many other ways. Nonetheless, we had no intention of neglecting the book-learning. An appropriate assortment of used textbooks was assembled as well as a generous supply of paper and writing implements, a new portable typewriter, and we even purchased a new encyclopedia set, since a good source of reference material would be vital.

The Canadian Consulate had informed us that British Columbia has a well established Government Correspondence School which serves children in isolated areas. We didn't know if we'd have any sort of mail service where we were going, so deemed it wiser to go prepared with home-tutoring materials.

After arriving and getting settled in at Manson, we sent to the Government Building in Victoria for correspondence work for Lynlee in grade eight and Leslee in grade six. It was required that we produce certificates from the last school attended and last year's work completed. All this was complied with.

When the work arrived, Lyn and Les excitedly tore into the packages. Before I could take time to supervise, they had the kitchen table strewn with textbooks, stapled booklets of assignment and teaching work, instruction sheets, French language records, paper and materials for Art work, and large envelopes for sending in their completed work. At first glance it looked like a formidable job ahead, but when it was all sorted out it consisted of Science, English Literature, English Language, Mathematics, Beginning French, Guidance and Health, and Social Studies for Lynlee. Leslee's elementary studies included Arithmetic, Literature (Reading), Language, Spelling, Social Studies, and Art.

Elementary School work is divided into three blocks of twelve weeks' work per block, for each grade. Les was sent the first block of twelve for a start, and being super enthusiastic, she attacked the work with great gusto declaring that it was a cinch. She had the first three weeks' worth done in one week, working only a short while each day. She incorrectly assumed that the whole block of twelve should be sent in at the same time instead of week by week. I hadn't even looked at the mass of material since both girls seemed to have everything under control and were not running into any snags. In fact, we were delighted to see them going ahead independently with what they knew was to be done. We didn't even have to designate any special school hours. It was working out beautifully. Of course books were dropped whenever anyone stopped by or anything of new interest was happening — which was *very* often.

By the end of December Leslee had skimmed through the first block of twelve and sent them in for grading. A month later, on the next mail day, she received the work back, graded, and orders to do it all over again using the new blank lessons enclosed, and to *"please do the work as instructed."* There was also a note to the Home Instructor (only then did I realize that I held that honoured position) to "Please supervise your child's work, read the instructions carefully, and see that the papers are done as directed."

Leslee was crushed, and I was mortified. The fun was gone. Now it would be work. After a couple of days of rallying myself for the new assignment, I sat down and gave the lessons a good looking over to see what she had done wrong. If I was mortified before, I was horrified to see what she had actually sent in. Her answers were all more or less correct. The biggest problem was the form the answers were to take. If they had said: "Use a separate sheet of paper for your answers" they meant just that. Les had written in margins, squeezed answers between printed paragraphs, overlooked a great deal, and in general had sent in papers badly done. I suddenly realized that we had been giving our eleven-year-old far more credit than should have been expected of anyone that age. Also it became very clear what was expected of the "Home Instructor."

A little of Leslee's spirit was broken with that first devastating blow, but with a lot of moral support and all the help I could possibly give her, we tackled lessons one through twelve over again. Fortunately everything didn't have to be redone, but fully three-quarters of it did. I started setting up each day's assignment for her, and by the time we were well into the re-run, she understood the precise form in which the schoolwork was to be presented: each separate sheet of answers must have her name, the subject, and the assignment number in the upper left-hand corner; on the right-hand side of the page the date must appear; skip two lines to begin the answers; number answers *outside* the left-hand margin; and so on.

By the time we got to the second block there was a warm-hearted note from the teacher stating her work was well done and she was enjoying having Leslee for a student.

Grades eight through thirteen were directed by the Secondary Correspondence Division. There were thirty-six lessons for Lynlee, too, but there were also examinations in each subject after each sixth lesson. It was required that we locate an "examination supervisor," preferably someone nearby, not a relative, who was a Canadian citizen. The obvious selection was Johnny, and he was willing. Subsequently, as Lyn neared the completion of each sixth lesson, a series of printed tests was mailed to Johnny. It was his job to be present while the tests were being written, allow the correct amount of time, and mail the tests back to Victoria in their special envelopes.

By the time winter had worn away and summer was approaching, neither of the girls had completed a whole year's work. In Correspondence schooling, fortunately, each student proceeds at his own pace and may begin his next year's work as soon as he has completed his present grade.

Wintertime Activities   17

The ability to use time wisely is a real talent. To be able to make living-in-the-North a successful venture is far more than a desirable talent. It's a necessity — a basic requirement for mental survival. Anyone can adapt himself to longer work periods if the cause is worthy, but the problems arise when the work period is over and free time begins. Here in the North there is no television to watch, no theaters, dances, shopping centers, no pubs to go to whiling away relaxing hours. There are no golf courses, skating rinks, playgrounds, or any commercial entertainment of any sort. During the isolation period which is half the year, daylight working hours are short, and evening leisure hours long. One should consider well how adept he is at worthwhile pastimes before deciding that this is the kind of life he wants. We didn't fully realize this ourselves before we came, but fortunately for us, leisure time pursuits were no problem.

It was here that our daughters discovered the world of books. Westfalls at Germansen had told us about the library-by-mail service, so we sent to the Prince George Library Commission giving our names, ages, and reading preferences. Each mail day about fifteen books would be sent in for our perusal. The librarians seemed to have genuine talent for picking excellent books to suit required tastes, and we had the opportunity of becoming acquainted with many authors whom we'd likely have missed altogether had we been doing our own browsing.

The girls began reading voraciously and for a few years were keeping a list of book titles and authors they had read. Leslee was almost to the hundred mark and Lyn past seventy when they began easing off on the enumerating. My first dilemma arose when I had to decide between tearing the kids away from an all-absorbing reading session to get at their schoolwork, or just let them read on. Usually I let them alone; but the lessons had to get done too. It was the formal schooling which suffered and the reading habits which thrived and grew. Back home in California the girls and indeed most all children never seemed to have time for free reading. We considered that after they'd been to school all day, the time before supper should be play time; then in the evening there was always the inevitable television versus homework hassle. Our way of life here afforded abundant reading time and this in itself was possibly the best educational advantage we could unwittingly have provided.

Artistic painting had never been more than a pastime with Larry but he was good at it, and Lyn had inherited some of this talent. She was adept at quick pencil sketches, and anything she attempted had the touch of a potential artist. The box of oil paints and watercolours, the canvas and easel were awaiting her eventual desire to experiment. Meanwhile, during that first winter Larry created an unusual work of art which caused considerable comment while it hung on our living-room wall. The frame is of one-inch saplings, varnished and held together with moosehide thongs. The "canvas" is a free-form piece of tanned moosehide with small holes punched around its perimeter, and lacings through the holes and around the pole frame holding the hide centered. The painted picture is a simple scene of mountains, river, cabin, trees, and sky. It all started as an experiment to see which media would work best on moosehide. Oils were tried in one area first, then pastel chalk in another section, then water-colours, even liquid embroidery and coloured felt pens. It's all there in one picture and is beautiful. All the colours have stood the test of time, and the picture is something I shall always treasure.

Robert was skilled at carpentry and when the mood would strike he'd put together a series of shelves or a clothes closet or a roofed-over front porch on their cabin. One evening he was whittling on a three-inch-thick section of small tree trunk and produced a deep ash tray which has proved utilitarian as well as clever. Instead of carving out the inside he burned it out in small sections with a hot poker. It required time, but that is one commodity we have plenty of.

Carolyn and I seemed to have the least amount of leisure but we got a lot of reading accomplished. I set up a primitive bookkeeping system for our small business and gave the photo albums and scrapbooks frequent face-liftings and up-datings.

Larry was an avid chess player and had belonged to a distinguished chess club in Los Angeles. Both the girls had played a fair amount of chess at school, so during the quiet winter months Larry began working with them to perfect their games. Leslee seemed to show the most promise in this field and she eventually became the "clearing house" for anyone who wanted a game with Larry. If they could beat her, then

Larry looked forward to a pretty fair challenge. Incidentally, over the years there were quite a few fellows who were chagrined to find themselves being bested by a young girl.

Immediately after finding the first jade boulder, and in anticipation of locating many more, we had purchased a rock saw. After all, if we were going into this jade business we'd want to go all the way with cutting, slicing, trimming, and polishing. The machine we had was a multiple unit with a six-inch diameter saw, a grinding wheel, and polishing disc. Unfortunately, the unheated back porch was the only area available for housing this machine so we couldn't work with it all winter. But as soon as the weather warmed up we decided to experiment with the piece of jade which Bruce and Bart had given us. Naturally the machine operated on electrical power, and fortunately our friend Tony had left a portable generator in our care with permission to use it freely. An inventory of gasoline stock indicated enough on hand to run the generator a little, so Larry took the lead in experimenting. He cut the entire piece of jade into ⅜″ thick slices. Most of these pieces went into the store for selling during the next summer, but Larry was eager to try his hand at doing up a cabochon, or ring-stone. He did quite well, but decided that he needed some professional tutoring before he could be satisfied with a finished product.

With the way of life as undemanding as it is, all sorts of fun-type things can happen spontaneously: snow-ball fights, dunkings in the snow, sledding at midnight. Very late one evening Robert and Carolyn came dashing over with a "let's make doughnuts" suggestion. We had no doughnut cutter but that fact only made the project more challenging since the idea had engendered so much enthusiasm. We used a glass for the first cut, and the opening of a bottle sufficed to cut out the holes. This operation was so much fun that the next night someone suggested making hand-churned ice cream. Unfortunately for the cleaned-up kitchen, that idea was a howling success too. From then on, however, I made a kill-joy ultimatum: no more late night cooking projects because of the big cleanup job next morning.

Northern Lights are a natural phenomenon visible in diminishing magnificence the farther south one is located from the North Pole. Spring and fall are supposedly the active seasons for the displays, but for some reason at our latitude we observe the greatest activity in the first part of the year.

One cold January midnight Lyn excitedly called us all outside to have a look. At first glance there seemed to be searchlights playing all over the heavens. In the next moment the scene changed and a shower of light would explode like a fireworks display. Then that was gone and there would be a series of undulating horizontal lines of light moving across the midnight blue. Next, a series of vertical streaks appeared from behind Wolfridge Mountain north of us, and these seemed to fade in and out as they moved across the horizon. The lights were mostly blue-white, but sometimes we'd see pastel pinks and greens. This display went on so long and was so ever-changing that we wanted to stay outside and not miss a bit of the show, but the temperature was against it. All we could manage was to stand outside for three or four minutes at a time, dash back to the stove for a warm-up, and then outside again. The exhibit went on for hours, so nobody got to bed very early that night.

The winter meat supply was usually acquired as late in the season as possible, and with the first moose we discovered that the killing was just the beginning. It took the best part of a week to accomplish the skinning, the quartering, the hauling in, hanging, cutting and wrapping. The average moose probably weighs seven or eight hundred pounds, so there's a lot of meat on a carcass of that size.

Robert and Larry felt that a picture of "How to Carve a Beef" would guide them into satisfactory results with their first moose operation. We cleared a work area, lined up cartons for the meat packages and tubs for the bones and scraps, got out freezer paper, tape, scissors, marking pens, and sharpened all the knives. Bob made the first incision in one of the hind quarters and soon lifted out a fine-looking chunk of roast. It took us a day and a half to carve up the four quarters, the huge rib sections, and the expansive meaty neck. We left the ribs until last, naturally, because the work is more tedious and less rewarding. All one gets is chunks of stew-meat, but there was a huge tub of it. Everyone had turns with the carving knives but Lyn and Les were most persistent. They didn't want to leave a shred of meat on a single bone.

We were meticulous with the carving job on our first moose and were duly proud of the neatly stacked and labelled boxes of meat packages set out to freeze. But inevitably, as time wore on and our experience with meat cutting became more commonplace, we settled for a limited number of cuts such as "Roast," "Stew Meat," "Steak," "Hamburger." The only exception was "Tenderloin" which we felt was justifiably worthy of special recognition.

After a few years had passed and several moose had gone through our skillets and roasters, we felt ourselves authorities on the cooking of this wild meat. Moose is tasty, but is often inclined toward toughness, so a little tenderizing action in the kitchen before cooking is advantageous. Steaks should *always* be cut to less than a half-inch thickness. Actually, the thinner — the better. This is best accomplished by slicing off the steaks when the meat is partially frozen (ice crystals still in the chunk). Commercial tenderizer sprinkled on before frying or broiling the steaks with onion rings assures a perfect entree.

Roasts should be sprinkled with tenderizer and cooked with bacon strips laid over the top. Bacon moistens the meat and adds a little fat to a product which naturally has little fatty tissue. Pot roast and "Swiss steak" were our favourites. For this we'd choose a large package of roast and cut off chunks of meat to whatever thickness was required.

The grinding of hamburger was the most monotonous chore of the whole operation, so it would be accomplished in one of two ways, depending on our mood. Sometimes we'd be industrious and grind it all up at the same time we had the entire meat-cutting mess around. Other times we'd decide to package up the chunks-to-be-ground into two or three-pound packages, freeze and store them, then thaw and grind a package of the chunks when we needed it. Although time-consuming, we found that it was advantageous to put the meat through the grinder twice. The first time through, most of the gristle and sinew wraps around the blades, making it necessary to dismantle the grinder for cleaning several times during one grinding. On the second time around a finer finished product is obtained and the remaining strings of sinew are completely removed. Also, on the second time through, we customarily grind in two or three strips of bacon which does wonders to the flavour and adds that little bit of fat which is desirable.

With meat-on-the-hoof so available, there is still only a limited number of animals taken by the residents during a winter. Technically, it is against the law; practically, we felt that we were not abusing the privilege. We used every bit of the meat and even saved the hide for tanning. King and other dogs in the area feasted on the bones.

We tried fishing through the ice but couldn't really call our efforts successful. The theory is that when the lakes and rivers have been frozen over for a few months, the fish have been without any new feeding material and should snap readily at anything offered through a hole in the ice. Much to our perplexity, however, they would bite only occasionally, and more often not at all.

Identifying tracks in newly fallen snow was another learning experience. Carolyn possessed a book which showed how to distinguish wild animals by their footprints and droppings. Eventually we spotted evidence of moose, caribou, wolf, fox, squirrel, snow-shoe rabbit, beaver, mink, martin, weasel, lynx, and wolverine.

The day after a particularly noisy wolf-howling night, we snowshoed out looking for tracks. Several wolves had followed the road right up the little rise onto the edge of town! The tracks were sharp and precise. Larry suggested making casts with some of the plaster of Paris we had brought for possible sculpting. This we did, and for comparison we also cast King's paw print. The wolves' were twice the size of King's! Since then, to our tremendous relief, we have learned that a wolf's feet do not relate to the overall size of the animal as a dog's feet do. Wolves are equipped with a very wide pad for walking over the crust of snow. That was a comforting bit of information.

One afternoon King started up a frenzied barking such as we'd never heard before. He raced from the front porch down the road to the edge of town, sounding the alert all the way. Les and Evy were the first ones out and halfway across the road to check out the problem, when Les shrieked, "It's a bear!" Grabbing Evy, she raced to the safety of the store. Robert snatched his rifle, and he and Larry cautiously made their way in the direction of the offender who by now had disappeared from immediate view. The rest of us stood outside but close to a door, should quick retreat be necessary. (We'd all heard the tale of the maddened grizzly who rampaged in the area a few years previously, and Johnny has a picture of a cabin with a gaping hole in the roof where the bear plowed through looking for food.)

Suddenly, to our horror, Larry and Robert came tearing back up the road yelling, "It's three grizzlies!" They dashed into the store, which happened to be the nearest available door behind which to protect themselves. We all figured we were being invaded, but after fifteen minutes and no invasion, we hesitantly ventured outside again. Robert took the lead in a wary investigation back down the hill. There were tracks showing that the bears had left the road and cut across to climb Wolfridge Mountain. A pair of binoculars revealed the three dark silvertips, clearly outlined against the snowy background, heading up and over the summit. Only after we'd all seen for ourselves did we relax enough to piece together the whole story.

Carefully scrutinizing the road and surrounding areas again, we found the tracks which indicated the bears had come down the hill in pursuit of a moose. King most likely saw the moose and went barking after it, thereby turning the moose off the other side of the road. But then he was facing the three bears! King's vicious, snarling warning turned the bears back down the road away from town, but he nipped one of them in the foot. As evidence there was a little fresh blood in the downhill bear tracks.

When the fellows had made their first cautious survey, they caught sight of the bears a short way down the road, pacing round and round and grumbling as if in pre-war pow-wow. When the bears spotted the men, however, they had all gone into action at once and started loping back up the road in pursuit. That was the occasion of Robert and Larry's record 220-yard dash. But instead of continuing the chase into town, the bears turned off the road and headed back home up and over the mountain.

Whew! That was one of our more exciting days!

Near the end of February of the first winter, and only two months after the shortest day of the year, someone observed that we had finished supper without having turned the lamps on. Spring was still a long ways off, but it was rather thrilling to realize that the worst of winter was already behind us.

About this same time Evy called our attention to a small black object moving around on the table among the dinner dishes. It was nothing more than a big lazy house-fly which must have been hibernating until the milder weather brought it out of hiding. It would take off and glide a few inches, then crawl a little ways, but it was listless for a fly. Evy was absolutely fascinated. He had been too small the year before to be concerned with such things. We cleared a path for the fly and watched it for a while before removing it to the outdoor world. It was amazing to suddenly realize that since the warm days of the previous summer we had, in truth, seen not one single crawling or flying bug, spider, or insect. This was our first fly in six months! What an awesome thing when we reminded ourselves of the constant battle against the summertime mosquitoes and the tiny, vicious black flies.

With six months between the shortest and longest days of each year, the change from eight to twenty hours of daylight is drastic this far north. Figured mathematically, it is an increase and decrease of approximately a half-hour each week, and it is noticeable. If the worst of winter had come and gone already, then living in the north country is a cinch. Well, let's say it's a challenge, but not a devastating one if approached with due respect and preparedness.

The Road is Open Again 18

With the advent of our first northern spring and the diminishing snow level, we began thinking actively about getting the place in readiness for the tourist season. There was much to be done in the store, the cabins, and in our own home.

Robert and Larry started with one of the rental cabins. It was a log building but the inside walls had been covered with cardboard, presumably for insulation against cold. Cautiously, one piece was pulled off, revealing two things: paper stuffing behind the cardboard, and also beautiful log surfaces. There was a brief consultation with Carolyn and me, and then the fellows went to work with gusto. Off came a flattened whole-kernel corn carton, and then a huge case which had once held cornflakes boxes. The only concession to propriety had been someone's nailing up the boxes with the printed sides to the wall. We had to admit it was an ingenious and inexpensive way to insulate, but there are other more modern ways which we preferred. Removing the cardboard revealed a couple more problems: a million shingle nails to remove, and the fact of daylight showing through many spaces between the logs. I think one entire day was devoted to nail-pulling.

The next job entailed cutting, limbing, and peeling about a hundred saplings which measured a diameter of one inch. Bits of moss, rag, and any other stuffing material we could scrounge was stuffed into the cracks, and then the saplings nailed down between each two logs. After varnishing all the surfaces, the total appearance of the inside was quite effective.

Carolyn and I rummaged through the cans and packages of new and partly-used paint which Mr. Hamilton had sold us. There was enough chocolate brown to cover a kitchen table and four sturdy chairs. After sending out an order for new linoleum floor covering, we checked over all the curtains in town until we could come up with enough of one type

83

to dress the three cabin windows. When everything was complete, we were quite pleased with a clean, rustic-looking interior. The other cabin wasn't too bad as it was. All we had to do there was match up curtains and re-hem them to proper lengths, and new linoleum was ordered here, too. Then we felt very good about both our rental cabins.

In the warehouse the packages of green powder paint had us perplexed for a while, so we mixed a little and brushed it on an experimental surface. It dried quickly and actually looked rather good, so Carolyn and I volunteered to brighten the interior of the store. Since the walls inside were completely lined with shelves, it was a tedious job. Each section of goods had to be removed as the paint brushes approached. The Trading Post was nothing but confusion for a few days, but the change in appearance was worth it all. I don't believe that store had been painted inside for at least twenty years.

Since our kitchen-living room is the setting for a great deal of coffee and conversation with guests all summer, it was agreed that this would be the next area to tackle. We started out one warm spring day by getting lots and lots of water heating on the stove. The grease and smoke film, which had emanated from two stoves for who knows how many years, took the four of us adults the best part of a day to scrub off, but afterward the nice clean walls were sorely in need of paint. Out came the catalogues again and we made up and mailed out an order for brushes, rollers, paint, and also for ten yards of curtain material which I had insisted upon. A month went by before the order was received. No time was wasted in applying two coats of paint to the entire kitchen-living room area, and in record time I had the four pairs of curtains cut, hemmed and hanging. Things were looking pretty good, if one didn't cast his eyes towards the floor. But the awful linoleum was there and in no way could be disguised. Even knowing there wouldn't be time to order, receive, and install a new floor before the activity of the summer season began, still we felt duty-bound to procure enough square floor tiles to do the whole room. When the tiles arrived some time later, we stacked the boxes neatly in a corner of the room awaiting just the right day when everyone was in the mood and things were quiet enough around town that we could move everything outside and go to work. Knowing our tendency towards procrastination, I worried a bit at the time, but to everyone's surprise the floor *did* get installed later on that same summer, and in a way that we could never have anticipated in our wildest imaginings.

Meanwhile, although not a trace of snow remained in sight of town, we knew that summits on the north road still held enough of the white stuff to prevent traffic through the Fort for a few weeks yet. Ice was completely gone from the creek and spring run-off water was inching its

The Owen family at the outset of their Manson Creek adventure.

Les and Lee provided country music . . . North Country style.

Without collar and license-tag King ran free in ideal dog country.

Small boy, big snowshoes. Evy was at home on the wilderness snow trails.

*Larry, Evy and the author, top center posed
with a typical hunting party from the south.*

It all began with Kelly 1 and Kelly 2, boulders of shining green jade. The first slabbing saw was simple and portable.

RIGHT – *At the beginning jade was coptered from field in dangling slings.*

Artistic Lynlee with jade pendant. She became proficient in the designing and making of jewelry.

Mount Ogden is known for its jade rock wherever jade is worked or sold. Taiwan receives most.

A boulder of solid jade, glacier moved and worn, must be carefully cut in place. Weight about 57 tons.

*Drilling and blasting yield jade from the seam in
glacially-eroded Mount Ogden.*

*The geology books studied at Manson Creek said such zones as
this where granite meets serpentine could produce jade. This one
did.*

A slabbing cut exposed the sea-green beauty locked within the rough exterior of this rock, much too big to be handled.

A field at Manson Creek was the setting for Lyn's wedding ceremony.

RIGHT — *The bride wore an especially ordered suit . . . after swift alterations by Mom.*

BELOW — *Steve and Les went 'Outside' for their wedding.*

way up the banks. The sun was moving higher in the sky each day, and it was good to feel that blessed warmth on exposed arms and legs again.

Carolyn and I spent many a morning sitting out front soaking up sunshine. One day it occurred to us that since we had such a large, bare front porch, it was a shame there wasn't any outdoor furniture to adorn it and make things more comfortable for lounging. The idea of a large porch swing hanging from the rafters seemed most attractive and a project we could handle. We both knew enough about our men, however, to know that we couldn't just ask for it and have it magically and spontaneously appear. In fact, we knew exactly how to get it accomplished and set about doing it.

Boards, rope, and tools were gathered together. We started measuring, sawing and hammering, and sure enough, it wasn't long before Robert sauntered over to ask what we thought we were doing.

"Oh, nothing," we answered. "Just trying out an idea." Robert went back to the motor he was working on. A short while later Larry walked by, paused, asked the same question and received the same reply. We pounded on.

As the seat and back were taking shape Robert could see what we were attempting. He came back once again to show us how there would be stronger support if we did it this way, rearranged things a bit, added side braces, and figured exactly where to drill the rope-holes for perfect balance.

By the time we'd fed the half-inch rope through the holes, knotted it under the seat and headed over to the porch with it, everyone was into the act. The men got it tied up to the rafters and there it was — a beautiful six-foot-long swing-seat with a slightly slanted back, and the whole thing adequate to support the weight and width of four adults. The swing faces out to the road and almost all the surrounding area of our town is visible from this spot. I'd hate to admit how many times Carolyn and I chuckled at our feminine wiles in bringing it about in the first place!

Bright daylight was extending itself to about ten o'clock those spring evenings, so after supper we'd wield rakes and shovels performing a town cleanup. During the time when the snow had been melting down we'd be surprised every so often by the appearance of a hammer, a wrench, a tire pump, balls, toys, innumerable objects which at some time during winter had been set down on a crust of snow, forgotten about, and suddenly covered by newly falling snow. But when the winter cover was all gone, there was six months' accumulation of rubble, soggy dead weeds, and all sorts of trash that didn't dissolve away with the disappearance of the disguising snow cover. Yes, indeed, spring thaw produces all sorts of surprises. Each night for a week or so we'd build a bonfire to dispose of the rakings and rubbish. It was an all-out effort with everyone considering it more fun than work.

But one evening when it was too soon to expect vehicles on the road, our work program came to an abrupt halt with the sound of a heavy piece of equipment off in the distance. An hour later, sure enough, a D-8 Caterpillar tractor came rumbling up the hill and into town, followed by a pickup truck with two men. They had "walked" the Cat the entire distance from the Fort, clearing all the deep snow areas in their path, and were eager to get their mining season off to an early start.

We sat around the big table with the three men as they ate the supper I hurriedly prepared for them, and they conversed enthusiastically about their plans for the summer.

It was good to see people from the outside again. We had now experienced a whole year of northern Canadian living; two seasons so different that one might think himself in different parts of the world in July and January.

During the 'People Time'   19

After a couple of years' experience we could say with certainty that the various facets of life and living in summer are as different to those of winter living, as night is to day, and that very fact keeps things from ever becoming monotonous. In winter there is the abundance of snow and cold, daylight hours are brief, there are practically no contacts with the outside world, and each resident has six months of time to pursue uninterruptedly just what he wishes. All the flies and mosquitoes are hibernating. Austerity of the season and winter freighting difficulties allow only a very limited quantity and type of fresh fruit and vegetables in the store. Mail comes in once a month.

The summertime six months period is exactly opposite in each of these features. The daylight hours are long, and sunshine is warm. Mail delivery now upped to once a week is staggering in its frequency. Fresh goods in the store is limited only by what we have failed to order. The little Trading Post begins to resemble a real store, with its shelves well stocked and the fruit table boasting a selection of apples, oranges, melons, plums, peaches, and other mouth-watering goodies.

The contrast which affects us most, however, is the coming and going of people who travel in and out and through our area. Customers and sales at the store and gas pump keep us intermittently at the beck and call of the public. This diversion is welcome because after the long winter of isolation and personal pursuits, the new stimulation from the outside feels good for a while. But in a few months this ever-present contact with people wears thin, and by the time October rolls around we are beginning to long desperately for the snow to fall and the road to close. Winter austerity makes summer freedom delightful, but with this freedom come demands on our time which make prospect of winter seem very desirable again. Both seasons are stimulating, and it takes the diversity to make it so.

"Expect the unexpected" is more than a motto for us; it is our summertime way of life. We never know when a household or working project will be interrupted. The wall of east windows on our house affords an unobstructed view diagonally across the road to the store front, so we don't find it necessary for someone to remain on duty during the day. There might be several hours between customers, but at other times there could be a continuous stream of tourists and conversations for an hour or two, or even for half the day.

The first few summers we devoted ourselves wholly to the business of "people." Newcomers were always interested in having a look around. They'd wander into the Trading Post, buy a few food items, and usually fill their car's gas tank from our almost famous, old-fashioned, hand-cranked gas pump. (By the middle of our second summer here we had installed an underground thousand-gallon gas tank with a hand-cranked pump and hose to deliver the goods. It wasn't until a few years and many comments and snap-shots later, that we realized the pump was one of a vanishing breed, and actually a desirable antique.)

We are an information center for the new visitors, answering the same questions over and over about how we found this place, how long we've lived here, if we *really* stay here year-round, what we do all winter, how cold it gets, how the kids get their schooling, how people make a living, what we do when we need a doctor, and so on. It is at this precise point that we have come to discover the difference in people, and only those who are in a business in which they contact the public day after day will understand what I mean. In our case, all the factors being discussed are constant, and the only variable factors are the people asking the questions. While everyone, hopefully, receives the same polite, friendly treatment, some people are just more fun to talk with than are others. Some would be granted ten or fifteen minutes of our time, while with others we'd feel privileged if they were interested in giving us an hour or two of their time.

About half the vehicles coming up the long road belong to people who have been here before or who do seasonal work in the area. For them Manson Creek is a place to stop and say hello, perhaps leave a message or pick up some item or message left for them by someone else, and invariably a place to have a friendly cup of coffee. For the individual with a flat tire on his car or leaking gas tank, or broken trailer hitch, Manson Creek is the first stop on the long road where tools can be supplied to the driver to do his own repair work. Many have had to learn all over again how to take a tire off a rim, take out the tube to patch it, get the tube back in the tire and the tire back on the rim, and finally to pump up the tire with a bicycle hand-pump. Things are done the slow, harder way here.

Each year when the road has opened naturally or when it has been plowed open, there will be a rush of mining people eager to get set up for another working season. The road and bridge foremen make their inspection trips to check on any winter damage and line up the summer work programs. The various freight men begin their hauling trips. Hunting guides of the area come in early to clear their trails and get all their camps set up. For several weeks it will be a bustling time of coming and going. And then the trailers and campers start rolling in.

The early weeks of every summer season are busy times and the following notes from one of the early scrapbooks concern that particular year, but are representative of the activity surrounding the opening weeks of every "people season."

Tuesday. Two Russell freight trucks arrived with our first big grocery order for the summer, and other supplies for people farther along the road. Along with Bruce was Don Gilliland of Germansen, back from the hospital after his freak gun-exploding accident which tore open his right arm and necessitated his being flown out. He required muscle and tendon repair, and fortunately will have almost full use of his arm. The men all had supper with us and helped Lyn eat her birthday cake.

Wednesday. Trucks began driving in, and much coffee and conversation ensued. The first convoy was a mining company that is taking trucks, men and machinery as far as the road goes, and then will travel by "Cat" for another two-hundred miles. They expect to arrive at their destination some time in July! They won't accomplish much more than to get there and get their camp set up this year.

Gene Jack and "Wes" Westfall stopped by on their way out to the big city to line up more mining equipment and supplies. They came in and talked a while and asked if they could pick up anything for us out in the city.

Bruce and Chet (Bruce's son-in-law) arrived back from Germansen and stopped in for coffee and to receive payment for the freight. We gave them the next grocery and gas order.

About 8:00 p.m. Larry Erickson's three white huskies were running around in the yard, but there was no sign of Larry. When he hadn't shown up an hour later, Robert took the truck and went down the road looking for him. Sure enough, there was Larry whom we hadn't seen since last year, "hoofing it" towards Manson. His truck had become badly entrenched in a mudhole about twenty miles back. We fed him supper and got him bedded down for the night.

Thursday. The extrication job required Bob, Larry O., and Larry E., plus the big Army truck and winch, and half a day's work. Erickson's truck was really bogged down.

Carolyn, Bob and the kids went fishing at Wolverine Lake this evening. Bob is the fisherman of the crowd. Everyone puts lines in the water in the same general area, and oftener than not, Bob is the only one who hauls in a fish. No one else even gets a nibble. This destroys my own personal opinion (untrained) about fishing and fishermen. I had thought that when the fish are hungry they'll bite on most anything, and for anyone; but if they're not interested in food, then nobody catches them. I'll have to revise my theory.

Friday. Larry and the kids went as far as the lake for a road cleanup. In three miles they picked up a truck-bed load of cans, bottles, paper scraps, old cartons, broken glass, and general litter which had been carelessly and unthinkingly strewn by our travelers of the previous summer and fall.

Evy fell and cut the side of his face on the edge of the porch. The cut wasn't too serious except that it was dangerously close to his eye.

The Department of Highways has passed a death sentence on one determined beaver whose efforts keep repeatedly causing flood problems in one particular spot on the road. Bob and Carolyn went with Jack Thomson to carry out the sentence, and then took a lesson in skinning as they watched Jack deftly peel the furry pelt off the executed offender.

Saturday. Five men from Vancouver in two trucks drove up to the store to ask for directions to Harley Polan's gold mine. They had just bought it, sight unseen, and of course didn't even know where it was. This seemed incredible to us, but it actually happened. The men had come in to get their camp set up and the operation started, but first they had to know where to go!

The road foreman stopped by for a visit before going on farther north. We always have a good time with him. He is over six feet tall, 220 pounds, and heavy framed, and he and Gene Jack who is about five inches shorter but weighs the same, have a perpetual contest going over who is going to lose ten pounds sooner. Each time Art makes a trip up to our area, he and Gene have a weigh-in at Gene's place, and then proceed to reward their vain efforts with a few bottles of beer.

Sunday. King got a big slash in one of his toe-pads, probably from an empty ham can in the dump. He's been leaving bloody footprints everywhere. Lyn and Les have been playing doctor, trying to keep a clean rag tied around King's foot. He's gobbling up all the attention and at the same time pulling all the bandaging off his foot. I guess nature will have to take over.

Ernie Floyd, one of our permanent summer residents and field prospector, appeared for this year's activities. He brought in for Leslee, our family's young rockhound, a ⅜" thick slice of rock which displayed an intricate design. Neither she nor any of us could identify it as a cross-section of petrified dinosaur bone from the Bad-Lands of Alberta.

A family who vacationed here last year returned and brought with them a generous box of beautiful big juicy Washington cherries for us, as well as a large bag of magazines and paper-back books which will be well perused.

Monday. Today we met and talked with two young Prince George businessmen. In the course of the conversation we learned that they had been children in Germany during the war years. They told us of scrounging for food, and of the terrible devastation and deprivation near the end of the war and just after. Twenty years ago these were innocent children of the enemy.

Here in Canada, unlike in Southern California, a large percentage of the population includes immigrants from other countries, so we often meet Austrians, Scandinavians, French, Ukrainians, and others of foreign birth. We find this most educational because we are as interested in what others have to offer as they are in hearing of our experiences.

Later in the day, Larry and Robert were recruited, along with others, to help clear the log-jam piled up for nearly one hundred yards back of the bridge at Germansen Landing. Already there is a two-foot bow in the bridge, and much concern is evidenced for its safety. Each year at high-water run-off time there is this danger, and sometimes it poses a real threat. The men may be working day and night for a week or more at untangling this mess.

These are not isolated experiences. Our scrap-books (one for each year we've been here) are crammed with daily notes on unique, humorous, pathetic, educational, and novel happenings and contacts with interesting and unusual people whose paths have crossed ours here in the far North. Neither are these occasional rare incidents. Almost every day from May to the end of October there is something of interest to read. Only rarely will appear the comment: "Relatively quiet day today."

'Water Witching' 20

A float plane circling town a few times and then heading to Wolverine Lake means that someone is flying in to Manson and needs a ride from the lake back to town. One day a private plane gave the signal, so we picked up on the cue and drove to Wolverine, wondering who it could be. There we met two fellows who wanted to spend a week at Manson, rent a cabin, hire a truck and driver, and prospect in the area. We brought them back to town and got them set up in one of our cabins. Then we arranged with one of the residents to drive them wherever they wished.

To say that the Owens are mildly curious would be one of the greatest understatements of the century. By evening of the second day we just knew we had to get to know these men better and find out whom or what they represented. So after supper Larry invited them over for coffee and pie (which I had conveniently whipped up that afternoon).

It was true that they were prospectors, but on a rather higher plateau. One owned and piloted the plane and was the president of the mining company which he represented. The other was the company's geologist, and the two were good buddies who had prospected together for a number of years. They both lived in Vancouver and were in their forties. One was married, and one single.

After that first visit they came over each evening for dessert and conversation. They talked "mining" and "jade" with Larry and Robert, and with the rest of us they discussed more personal matters. George volunteered that he was certainly going to bring his wife along on the next trip, vowing that he was sure she'd love our family and we'd probably love her too.

During the coffee session on the last day of their stay, we got onto the subject of a piped-in water supply. We discussed all the various systems we'd already thought of, and George enthusiastically informed us that he knew how to "witch" for water and might be able to locate the best place for us to sink a well. Naturally we all laughed, as did George's partner, Bud.

Undaunted, George solemnly requested, "Lynlee, would you get me a couple of wire coat hangers?" The hangers were produced and George opened them up into long, straight lines, cut off the twisted ends, bent the last four inches of each one to right angles forming handles, and then said, "Come on!"

He headed out the door with all of us following, laughing. This behaviour of George's was new even to his long-time partner. As we tramped around in the 2.2 acres which comprised the deeded ground area of Manson Creek, George was leading the procession and holding the two wires by the short handles with the long lengths parallel and pointed directly ahead of him.

"When we walk over a good underground water supply the wires will swing across each other and I won't be able to control them," George said, determined to prove his ability. We continued parading around until suddenly, "Zing!" the wires swung across each other. All eyes bugged out as George backed up and approached the spot again, with the same result. We stopped laughing but still weren't convinced that there wasn't some trickery involved.

"O.K., so you can do it. Let me try, George," said Larry stepping forward to demand the wires. He went back about twenty feet and approached the same spot again, holding the mysteriously performing objects in front of him. Suddenly they swung across each other and nothing Larry could do would restrain the action. He was stupefied.

"I still don't believe it," he insisted as he continued walking all around with the wires, but purposely avoiding the right spot and looking for a reaction somewhere else. Nothing much happened until he walked over to the right spot and then again, zing!, over went the wires. Larry shook his head in disbelief at what he couldn't explain.

We all had to give it a try in turn. Bud walked over the spot and not a thing happened, which is exactly what he expected. Then I tried it and it worked for me. Each of us tried in turn and it worked for some and not for others. For a check, Larry took the wires and walked over a known underground stream from Johnny's well to another well down closer to the creek. He zig-zagged back and forth with the wires crossing and un-crossing, tracing the underground system all the way. That particular water route was off our property, however. We were looking for water within our own boundaries and George's discovery seemed to be the best one.

That day we decided something about "water-witching" or "dousing" as it is "scientifically" called. Since it works strongly for some people and not at all for others, the mystery must involve individual body electricity or chemistry as it reacts to the electricity or chemistry of the water and the ground being tested. Incidentally, dousing never works over surface water. All these little points add to the intrigue of the action.

We never did dig down to find out if there really is water there. Someone started once and got down about four feet before giving up; but we knew if we ever decided to dig a well, that would certainly be the first spot we'd seriously try.

A few weeks later George's plane circled town again, and this time our water-witcher was accompanied by a beautiful young oriental lady, about half his age.

My first thought when I saw them was, "Why George, you ol' rascal, you." But then he introduced Tamae, his bride of two years. We were thrilled to meet her. She had married George in Japan and had come to Vancouver to live his kind of life, leaving an exalted position with an oriental air line company as airport hostess to travelling V.I.P.'s. We had a wonderful time with her while George was out prospecting. She and Carolyn and the girls and I sat around day after day talking and sharing experiences. Hers were far more exciting than ours, we thought, because hers were so different — a whole new world to us. We heard some fascinating tales about the Very Important People of the political and entertainment fields who had passed through the airline waiting-rooms of Tokyo.

To our ever-growing list of new friends we added Bud and George and Tamae. Somewhere I have read that there are no strangers in the world — just friends you haven't met as yet. We were fortunate in meeting new friends day after day, every summer, every year.

Jade Hunting 21

For two years each approaching summer would find Larry and Robert busily making verbal and practical plans for the seasonal jade prospecting at Kwanika Creek. Trucks would be put in readiness, camp gear assembled, needed items listed and checked off. There would be tents, camp stoves, flashlights, sleeping bags, dishes, pots, rock picks, hip-waders for splashing around in the creek, lots of extra pants and sox, and an abundant supply of easily prepared food. On each morning of departure it seemed to take every one of us, all running errands in different directions, to get the two men and trucks on their way. I, personally, breathed a sigh of relief when they were off. Carolyn usually gulped down a few sobs since she was not yet accustomed to being separated from her husband.

Kwanika Creek is located about fifty miles west of Manson, so each excursion was planned for at least a week's stay. The first trip each year, however, was usually too early and the fellows would have to return the same day they had left. In eagerness they would have arrived before the high water had subsided. Spring run-off in all the rivers and creeks of the north country is an awesome affair. Waters rise to three or four times their normal depth, inundating the banks and sometimes washing out, or at least threatening, the bridges. The cresting and diminishing of different waterways varies each year, so if Larry and Robert found their jade creek too high, there was simply nothing to do but return home and try again in a week or two.

Eventually, however, camp would be set up and serious prospecting begun. The fellows would spend their days looking up and down the creek, in the water and in the banks. Finding a good jade boulder is a chancy thing. On the outside its crust may be an oxidized black or brown, a dry powdery white, or very rarely an unmistakable smooth green. Shapes of the rock will vary, but a flattened pear-shape is typical if anything is. Sizes of the rocks will range from a few pounds to many tons. Because of the terrific tumbling force of the rushing spring high waters, new boulders may be exposed to view each year.

It didn't take long for our hardy prospectors to discover that it would be a great boon to have a camp cook and dishwasher. The only problem in filling this vacancy was in choosing one of the many willing volunteers. All of us at home were eager to see this new area which was commanding so much attention. Carolyn was the logical first choice and she accompanied the men for the next few trips. But it wasn't long before Lyn began trying to convince everyone that she, too, could put together a meal — especially their quick cooking, can-opening kind. All she really had to learn was how to juggle pots on the two-burner camp stove in the correct order so as to have everything done at the same time. Since it was only her father and Robert she was feeding, Lyn didn't suffer too much from inadequacy pangs during her first few attempts. The next summer Leslee was added to the lineup of revolving cooks. Indeed, going to Kwanika was considered a vacation experience away from the life at Manson which was also almost one big holiday most of the time. After meals and dishwashing, the cook could accompany the men up and down the creek, go fishing, hunt fancy rocks or artistic driftwood, paint or sketch a picture, read, write letters, sunbathe, or do just whatever might seem desirable at the moment.

Although other people also held placer leases along the same creek and were looking for the same rock we were, we seemed to have the best two-mile, four-lease stretch of the waterway. The fellows found more and better jade than their neighboring lease-holders either because the jade was just there to be found, or because they had more time to spend looking for it. All during the summer others would be dropping in to spend a few days or a week of their holidays, hoping to find one good piece of jade to make their efforts worthwhile. But Larry and Robert had a distinct advantage in actually living close enough to be able to spend a lot of time prospecting often and thoroughly each summer.

Bruce Russell, our freighter, and his partner, Bart Reil, would drop in to Bruce's leases down the same creek, as often as their working days permitted; but before long Bart, who is an avid collector and dealer in jade, became aware that Larry and Robert were the jade finders. In the natural progression of events, Bart eventually became our agent. We'd contract with Bruce to haul the boulders back to his own yard in Fort St. James where the big circular diamond saw cut the rocks into twenty-pound chunks. Then Bart would take them to his home in Prince George, cut the chunks down to smaller pieces, grade them, and make his contacts for sales. This arrangement was quite successful, and with the profits from sales the first few years we bought our first generator for electrical power, a snowmobile for winter fun, a radio-phone for that security feeling in times of possible emergencies, a rock drill for taking samples from boulders, one of our $2000 winter grocery orders, and other miscellaneous wants and needs.

Successful as this arrangement was, still we felt we were missing a big part of the excitement by having someone else do the cutting of the rocks. There is no small thrill involved in getting that first look when the saw finally has ground its way through a thick jade boulder and the two halves are exposed to human view for the first time in the eons of years which represents the age of the rock. The anticipatory wait is not unlike that of parents having the first look at their newborn baby after the long nine months' period. The analogy ends with the first look, however. If the inside of the rock is no good, or less than the drill core led them to expect, it may be discarded.

So, in short order we had our own rocksaw. It was set up in the yard adjacent to our house. A six-horse motor ran the 36″ diameter, diamond-studded blade, and a supply of water was rigged up for running a steady stream into the cut as the blade ground its way through the rock. Three or four hours were required to make one cut through a twelve-inch thickness of rock, so this was no speedy operation. Big boulders required several cuts. It was necessary for someone to monitor the operation at all times to make sure the blade didn't get jammed in the cut, or the water stop flowing for even a few minutes.

Naturally, this open-air jade cutting afforded a new attraction for tourists driving into town. Almost invariably they would stop to watch and ask and talk. Most everyone had heard of jade, but very few had ever seen it or even knew that it was being found in this north-central part of British Columbia.

Before long, however, word of Kwanika Creek jade and its Manson Creek association began to spread. To the majority of rockhounds, jade is one of the "ultimates" in rock hunting, so when Kwanika jade began appearing on the market and its location inevitably became known, rockhounds and other mining people began drifting into the area. By the end of the second summer on this creek, Larry and Robert were already feeling that they had exhausted most of the possibilities of their two-mile stretch. A new friend, a geology professor from an Alberta University, was advising them, with considered evidence, that since Kwanika was located within a wide serpentine belt, other creeks within this same geological formation might be jade-producing too. Our men wasted no time. They made immediate plans for moving their camp to another area which would be advantageous for prospecting a number of creeks within a thirty-mile radius.

We had all felt kindly toward Kwanika and it had been good to us. But as soon as the tents and campers and trailers started moving in, and the rockhound clubs began taking field trips to our creek, then it was too much. Time to move on. But we were not losing interest in the jade business, or moving out of it. Most certainly not! We were becoming more deeply involved in it than ever.

Those first few years of jade mining we saw Bart Reil as often as he could manage to be away from his automotive business. Bart gave Larry some lessons in making jade into beautiful jewelry stones, or "cabochons". They spent a good deal of time working with the saw-grinder-polisher unit in the back room. Before long Larry's lapidarian techniques were well on the way to perfection.

To make a "cab," one slices off a ⅜" thick slice of jade, chooses a nice clear area and marks out the shape of the stone to be cut. The slice is held in the hand and fed into the trim saw until rough cuts outline the shape of the stone. After that the grinding begins; coarse grinding belts are used first and then the finer ones. A polishing agent is applied for the final shine. It's an easy process to talk through and demonstrate, but for perfection in performance, experience is required.

Larry's leisure evenings one winter were spent in practising this art of doing up a perfectly shaped and polished ring-stone. After he had the technique down pat, he began teaching Leslee. She learned the process but never pursued it to the point of becoming an artist in the field. Lynlee learned later and became so adept that she surpassed her father in jade-polishing perfection. We thought of creating a section in the store for handmade jewelry to enhance the shelf of rough cut blocks of jade for sale. Perhaps this idea might become reality some day but someone was going to have to get busy and start producing.

Through Bart Reil we met a woman who is a jewelry artist in western Canada and who has demonstrated silver-smithing on television. She is also vitally involved with jade, so it was inevitable that our paths would cross; and they did. We became well acquainted with her husband and family during numerous rock-hounding trips up to the Manson area. She volunteered to introduce us to the art of silver-smithing, and on one of her visits brought a portable supply of necessary tools, silver sheet, silver wire, and soldering equipment. Larry was the first student of this new art, so the next winter silver as well as jade provided the extra-curricular activities in the back workroom, which by now had been completely insulated and equipped with a woodstove. Now that we had so much interesting material to work with, this room was becoming our creativity center.

Summer is a Busy Season 22

After only a few years we could see the pattern of activity during "people time" evolving. Our life here every day in summer could be likened to the hectic weekend of a city family when everyone is at home, in and out of the house all day, neighbors in for coffee, Dad trying for a nap, odd jobs being done around the house and yard, meals all off schedule, and general confusion being the order of the day.

Things are not quite as hectic as that because when this type of scene is the everyday way of life, the confusion mellows and people and actions have a way of falling into a routine of sorts. The only uncontrollable component is the not knowing when the next car will drive into town, and what will be required when it does. For example:

Sunday. There have been five trailers and campers parked in and around the yard last night and today. The caravan is moving on tomorrow, but today the kids have all been having fun playing volleyball and hiking around together. They've had campfires each evening. Lyn and Les make good junior hostesses.

Monday. Bruce delivered a propane refrigerator for the store. Arrangements for purchasing this item had been made through a newly-met friend who works in a Prince George furniture store but was making a sight-seeing trip up this way. He had promised to let us know when a good used gas fridge became available. This is certainly not the way we have bought furniture or appliances in the past, but the arrangement worked out well in this case. The refrigerator is in excellent condition.

Rented a cabin to a geology professor and two lively young students, all from McGill University in Quebec. They are going farther into the mining country tomorrow, but tonight we all had an enjoyable and educational session around our table.

Tuesday. Exciting helicopter activity today. A mining company is flying in its men and equipment. The "chopper" has made about four trips in and back out again from Manson, setting down and taking off in our front yard.

A young man drove up to the store and asked if this was the Manson Creek Ghost Town! At my obvious astonishment, this visitor produced a book entitled "Ghost Towns of British Columbia" by Bruce Ramsey, which does, indeed, have a chapter devoted to the 1869 gold rushes in this Omineca country. Both Manson and Germansen had been overnight "flash in the pan" bustling towns of several thousand fortune hunters. Within two years there was scarcely anyone left. At the present time there is nothing to see of the old buildings except for a crumbling foundation here and there. I suppose that compared with what our part of the country was a century ago, we could be considered ghost towns now. But there are certainly times when the "ghosts" are so active that there aren't enough hours in a day to accomplish what needs doing. "Ghost Towns" — hummm?

Wednesday.   One of the road men brought his two boys along to play with Evy, while he travelled on to Germansen. We hadn't realized how routinized and predictable Evy's activities and wanderings actually had become, and how at ease we were in our knowledge that he was always not far away. Today we had to locate the three adventurers several times. I think we shall have to discourage this all-day child care. It is not conducive to peace of mind during these busy summer days.

Lyn, Les and Evy go berry-picking frequently now, with home-made jam and dishes of fresh berries as the goal. There are several varieties up here: raspberries, tiny wild strawberries, blueberries, huckleberries and cranberries.

Two young brothers are in for the summer, doing assessment work on a placer lease a couple of miles up the road. They have a pump and sluice box set up and are working every day. Most evenings they walk down to town to visit and play badminton with the girls.

Thursday.   Rick Daley, boss of a small mining crew working a few miles away, brought up a projector to show the motion pictures he had made last year of Manson Creek and of us, of our jade cutting, and of his own mining activities. He and his workers are frequent visitors in town, which really means that they are good friends of the family because when they come to town there is nothing to do except go to the store or visit with the store owners. Rick brings in a few machines and a small crew each summer, hoping to locate a streak of "paydirt."

This afternoon we met a professor of psychology from the University of British Columbia. Larry and I both warm up immediately to people in the field of education. Larry "talks the same language," and I've listened to it so long that I feel myself a kindred spirit. It was easy to surmise that this man's classes must be popular ones because he seemed such a personable fellow. He was intensely interested in us and in the way of life we were providing our family. Our jade project fascinated him so much that he gave Larry an order for a pair of jade earrings to be made for his wife. This was the first actual jewelry order Larry had had, and it proved to be only the beginning.

Friday. We had one of our busiest days at the store. There must have been twenty cars and trucks stop here ar various intervals during the day. "Twenty" doesn't sound like a traffic jam, I know, but it turns out to be just that when almost every family stays around for an hour or so.

In between store visitors, we were frantically trying to get Robert and Larry off for another few days of jade prospecting.

Saturday. Three young mining fellows came to town for a casual visit which turned out to be an all night affair. Carolyn, Lyn, Les and I sat around the kitchen table with them the whole evening, laughing, joking, nibbling popcorn and cake, drinking coffee, and finally got to telling all the horror stories and scary movies we'd ever seen or heard about. By three o'clock in the morning everyone was too keyed-up and terror-stricken to head off toward their own individual cabins, so we decided to fix a *very* early breakfast. When that had been accomplished, dawn was breaking and all the fearful shadows had vanished.

*   *   *   *   *   *

Although we didn't know it when we got up one particular September morning, this was going to be the day for laying the new floor tiles which had been stacked in one corner of the room for a few months now.

We were entertaining three gregarious hunters whom we'd invited for coffee. They really were lots of fun, even though we knew part of their liveliness was inspired by the bottle which was in evidence. They called it the fourth member of the party, and brought it in with them for the purpose of making our coffee more flavourful.

Suddenly, for some inexplicable reason, Evy picked one of the tiles from the top of the pile and brought it over to the table.

"See our new floor," he chirped, as he presented the tile to Frank.

"So you've going to have a nice new floor, are you?" Frank responded.

I intruded into the scene and told them that as soon as we could see our way clear to turn the room upside down for a day, we'd get the new tiles down over this horrible flooring.

"Eric just did his kitchen floor last month, didn't you, Eric?" Bill commented. Eric nodded assent as he took another swallow of his spiked coffee.

"You know what, guys?" said Frank, addressing his companions. "We ought to put this floor down for these nice people." Everyone responded at once, but their enthusiastic "Sure, sure!" was more determined than our "No, no!" The more they thought about it, the better the idea became. We told them they couldn't possibly use up their holiday in drudgery. They assured us it would only take a few hours, and had practically started moving furniture outside already.

They took over in masterful fashion, calling for plywood for the base (which fortunately we had), and gathering together all the necessary tools and bottles, they set to work. When they were three-quarters of the way across the long 22' x 12' room, enthusiasm was showing signs of waning, and the bottles were all empty. I was keeping an unobtrusive eye on things, but they were still lining up the colour designs in the tiles properly.

It took longer than they had estimated of course, and as darkness was approaching we urged them to leave it and we'd put in the last five rows. But no, they had started the job and were determined to finish it. I have to admit they were good sports about it and saw the job through to the end, but they were showing unmistakable signs of being very relieved when they staggered to their feet and left.

The new floor looked magnificent! We were delighted to have it all accomplished so unexpectedly, and were completely overwhelmed by the unheard-of generosity of these new friends. Knowing us and our habits of procrastination, I could venture to guess that those boxes of tiles might have sat right where they were through that whole summer and fall, and on through winter until the warmer weather of the next spring would allow working with the doors open and the furniture moved outside.

*　　*　　*　　*　　*　　*

Along with all the strangers we'd meet for the first time each summer, and the returning vacationers we'd seen previous years, there were a number of men whom we would see often during each "people time." These would be individuals whose particular line of work would bring them up into our area for one reason or another.

The Conservation Officer, or "Game Warden" as he is more commonly called, would arrive unexpectedly and usually stopped in for coffee before going on up the road. He always had an incident or two to relate about his latest pile of confiscated rifles taken because they were being carried, loaded, in moving vehicles. Another time he was beaming all over while telling us about the arrest of a group of men who had set up camp at Germansen Lake and were netting fish after dark. It's completely illegal to net fish, it's illegal to have the hundreds of pounds of fish which they had taken, and their planned program of selling these fresh-frozen trout to city restaurants at a handsome profit also had a black-market smell to it. As a result of the court case the men lost their trucks, which carried cleverly concealed deep-freeze units, their boats, all their elaborate fishing gear, and on top of everything else were required to pay heavy fines. We congratulated the Game Warden roundly on that victory. There had been evidence and suspicions that some people had been doing this very thing for the past two summers.

On another occasion the Warden told us about one of his "plain clothes" camping trips which he was still chuckling about. The occupants of a nearby tent had been taking turns with the binoculars and were concentrating on something across the lake. Being the friendly sort, our hero sauntered over and inquired what they were looking at.

"There's a beauty of a moose over there on the hill. I'm thinking about rowing over and getting a shot at it," replied the unwary camper.

"I wouldn't if I were you," the Warden said, producing his badge. "It's still two days until the opening of hunting season."

"Oh, good God, I meant get a shot with the camera," the man hastily recovered. "I wouldn't dare shoot a moose this early."

*   *   *   *   *   *

A regular visitor every summer is the Department of Mines Inspector from Victoria who is in charge of the "grub-stake" program. Each year, those who apply and who can pass a test of identifying a certain number of selected mineral specimens, are granted summer financing for the purpose of going out into the mining area of their choice to prospect. So this Inspector spends his summers touring the mining areas in the province checking on his individual prospectors, not only to see that they are doing the job, but also to be helpful in any way possible. He passes through the Manson-Germansen area each year and always stops in for a sociable visit.

Another representative from the Department of Mines is concerned with safety and legality of any mining operation. He is the one who is called in to arbitrate any disputes over staking or boundary lines of claims. He, too, always stops in to see us and indulges in a cup of coffee or occasionally a meal at our table.

*   *   *   *   *   *

Seen frequently on the roads during summer months are the Forestry trucks and jeeps. Brush and tree fires caused mostly by electrical storms are common in and around our one-hundred-mile radius of activity. Almost every year there are numerous small fires, and sometimes one will rage out of control. At one time one of the major fires in the province was racing through brush and timber 150 miles northwest of us, and creating a flurry of activity. Men and equipment were constantly being moved through to the fire lines or being flown in and radio-phones were crackling with messages and instructions. Every evening the setting sun, as seen through the heavy smoke haze, was an unbelievable dark magenta-red, and the clouds on the surrounding horizon looked as though they, too, were on fire.

Another year there were three fires burning concurrently in different nearby areas, and this time we really experienced a hubbub of feverish activity on the part of the Forestry Department.

Since there are so many fields of action each summer during the high fire-hazard season, each fire will be given a name, somewhat in the way that hurricanes are named. There seems to be no particular system for naming. Sometimes the area name will be utilized, as "Usilika Fire" or "Kwanika Fire." Sometimes descriptive terms are used, such as "Ready Fire," "Out-Of-Hand Fire," or "Grow Fire." But whatever the nomenclature, once it's given it is official, and whenever that name is used every forestry man and fire-fighter knows which fire is being referred to.

*   *   *   *   *   *

By our third summer here, the business and activity in our whole northern area necessitated more frequent and more regular freight and mail service. Consequently, the Russell Transfer trucks appeared at least once during every week with a load of groceries, fuel, mail, and sundry supplies. Usually Bruce Russell, himself, would handle this northern haul, but sometimes one or another of his crew of drivers who work in and around the home base in Fort St. James would bring in the load of goods.

Another fast-growing freight and bus service is Alex Mitchell's Fort St. James Stage Line which comes in on Thursday and goes back on Fridays each week. Alex started with a once-a-month taxi run up here. Then he obtained a larger van-type vehicle for carrying people and a little freight each week. The last few years he's needed a crew-cab truck with a large, high, box-enclosed truck bed. Business is good and getting better as the country continues to open farther and farther north of us.

*   *   *   *   *   *

The postmaster in the Fort holds a supervisory position over the small post offices in this northern area. Once a year he comes up for auditing purposes. But after the work is finished he stays a while longer and gets in a bit of fishing and fun, thus combining business and pleasure.

*   *   *   *   *   *

Off and on all summer we will see the road and bridge crews. These men are responsible for keeping the stretch of road between the Fort and points north in good driveable condition. Since ours is a dirt road, it must be graded once or twice, and ruts filled in, each year after the snows have gone. Usually the grader goes over the whole stretch of road once again sometime during the summer. Some of the bridges and culverts will need to be repaired or replaced, and brush must be cut back from the edges of the road where it tends to overgrow and cause hazardous conditions. At least one bridge is completely rebuilt each year.

Everyone who drives in over this long graded unpaved highway invariably has some comment to make about the experience. Either: "The road is better than I've ever seen it," or "Heavens! that road is terrible. Why don't they do something about it?" It took us a while to figure out why we could hear such opposing comments from different people all in the same day. The answer lies in just what each individual was expecting when he started in from where the pavement ends. If he was completely unused to dirt roads and thought it would be a terrible, but necessary trip, then it might not have turned out so bad. But if he was expecting to breeze right along, then he might have been in for some real surprises.

But everything considered, the road and bridge men are on the job. I find it difficult to recall more than one or two times that the road was closed for any twenty-four hour period (in summer) due to a bridge wash-out or break-down, or some other problem along the way.

*   *   *   *   *   *

The branch of the Welfare Department which includes this northern area is located in Vanderhoof, and for many years John Busby was its director. Whenever a business trip brought John up into the Manson-Germansen territory, he would make a pleasure trip out of it and bring along his wife and family. They would camp out in the yard with a tent and sleeping bags, cook and eat outdoors, and the family would fish or hike around while John attended to whatever business had brought him up. Every night a campfire would lend its cosy atmosphere to marshmallow-roasting, story-telling, idle conversation, or group singing. John's hearty, confident voice would boom over the others in such an experienced manner that I asked him where he had sung before. After a little demurring, he admitted that years ago he had done some singing and announcing on a radio station in the East.

John and Ruth had two older daughters and a young son, just as we did, but they also opened their home and their hearts to homeless youngsters. Sometimes their "adopted" children stayed only a night or two while a more permanent situation could be worked out. Sometimes the visits lasted a few weeks, and sometimes even a few years. Whenever we saw them they always had one or more extra youngsters besides their own family, and as far as we could tell, all were treated equally, respected, disciplined, and trained equally. The Busbys had a lovely house, and even more important, a beautiful home. They were both strong, forceful personalities, and gave of themselves unstintingly. If I were ever to have nominated a candidate for "Citizen-of-the-Year" award, this energetic and warm-hearted couple would have been my choice without hesitation. In the four years that we knew them, before John was transferred from the area, our opinion of him and of his wife never wavered from our very first impression of them. We had never met any couple who were so lovingly and unselfishly dedicated to helping the less fortunate and helpless.

Broken Partnership 23

About the time everything was looking good and possibilities for prosperity seemed right around the corner, Robert and Carolyn began thinking it was time to move on. Here was where we were faced with a dilemna. We Owens were involved and happy with our life here and had no desire to leave. Yet, at the time we bought Manson Creek we had all mutually agreed to do some fixing up for a few years and then sell out and divide the profits. When this pact was made we had no idea what an abundant and fulfilling life the place could provide.

Our partners being considerably younger and not quite ready yet to settle down, perhaps even a little homesick, had decided between themselves that they wanted to go back and pick up where they had left off. We had a conference and decided that we would stay, but would pay our partners half of everything the fellows had earned together here. This decision created the second dilemna because everything they had earned had been poured back into the improvement of Manson Creek and expansion of stock in the store. No one had any personal bank accounts. We had another conference within the family as to how to come up with several thousand dollars. Larry's solution was for him to seek a teaching job in Fort St. James for the coming winter, if Bob and Carolyn would agree to stay on while he was gone. A man around the place is vital, and especially during winter.

This seemed a pretty drastic solution. A whole winter without Larry here . . .! But he reasoned that he could drive up and back many weekends in September and October, and he could fly in for the Christmas and Easter holidays. And before too long the temporary separation would be all over and its purpose accomplished. Since I couldn't come up with a better solution I had to agree.

After mailing an application to the local school district, and after sending to California for photostated copies of his teaching credentials, only then did Larry confess to me that he'd found the winters here a little more confining and stifling than he had expected, and maybe a winter spent working and earning money for a worthy cause would actually be a restorative measure. He assured me that he loved Manson Creek almost as much as I did, and certainly the jade-mining potential was too good to ever consider leaving this place.

I cringed at his confession. Was this the same Larry who had always wanted to get away to some deserted spot in order to be free to paint, write, relax or work, throw away the clocks and just *live?* Using his own logic, summers should have been the times he dreaded, and winter solitude the lovely period for creativity. His unspoken thoughts came through loud and clear, and I began wondering if our days at Manson Creek were numbered.

In due course the official acceptance was received from the local school district and Larry was assigned to teach a Grades Four and Five combination class. Someone suddenly realized that here was the perfect opportunity for Lynlee to go along with Larry and get in another year at public school. She would have a place to live and could also be responsible for a little light housekeeping and cooking for the two of them. Lyn was ecstatic! For some time she had been bogged down and depressed by the heavy load of work demanded by the Correspondence School. A year back in "civilization" would be just what she needed in the way of a lift.

Larry took one trip to the Fort during summer to get something lined up in the way of housing. That turned out to be a problem because there was nothing for rent. Building speculation had not yet reached this far north, but one far-sighted resident was in the process of building a six-unit motel. The owner-builder thought he could have the first two-bedroom unit completed by September first, so as a last resort, Larry secured that for himself and Lyn. Actually, he had planned to live as modestly as possible and a brand new, all electric, furnished, lake-view apartment seemed more than he needed. But inexplicably, the rent was extremely reasonable.

When September rolled around, Lyn and Larry departed on their adventure, leaving Leslee, Evy and me to handle things in Manson Creek, with Carolyn and Robert's help. Hunting season had opened so the store and gas pump were bustling scenes of activity, and there were enough people around that we didn't get that lonesome feeling for a while. Besides that, Larry and Lyn did return on several weekends, driving up and back the 120 miles until winter snowfall closed off the road.

Early in December Larry wrote suggesting that we have a family reunion out there for Christmas. There would be plenty of sleeping

108

room (two double beds, and Evy on the sofa), and we could have fun together at a time when families should be together. Leslee's reaction, upon reading this, was a tremendous "Whoopee!" She immediately began working out all the details. We could ride out the next mail-day with Bruce in his wintertime vehicle, the SnoCat. Bob and Carolyn would be around to take care of the limited store business and mail for a month. I agreed that there didn't seem to be any reason why we couldn't, so we began making immediate plans.

The 120 miles to the Fort by SnoCat is a long, slow trip at an average of eight miles per hour. The machine is reliable and comfortable, however, with a cab large enough for six people. After fifteen hours of travel we arrived at our destination, laden with luggage for a month and the gifts which had been ordered early and had already come in to Manson by mail. We even took along the tree-trimmings which we'd accumulated by that time, and also a seven-foot absolutely perfect Spruce tree which Bruce obligingly tied onto the top of the vehicle. It was wonderful to see Lyn and Larry again, and enjoyable to live for a while in their lovely apartment complete with all the "modern conveniences" we'd learned to do without.

During the time we were there, we witnessed a rare spectacular early morning show. Through our east windows the sky and clouds were bathed in blood-red reflection from the sun which was just peeping over the low hills. We stood there admiring this glorious sight for quite a few minutes. Then, to let the new day in, Evy pulled the cord which opened the drapes covering the west windows. To our delighted astonishment, there was a huge, full, yellow moon about to drop below the west horizon across the lake. Its brightness was reflected over the frozen surface of the lake, as well as onto the clouds in the western sky. We stood transfixed gazing first through the east then through the west windows. It was a fantastic display. I have no idea how often this phenomenon occurs, but we enjoyed thinking that we were witnessing something rare.

It was in Fort St. James that both Lyn and Les seemed to have problems in finding things to do. With recreations of one's own devising the only way things are done at Manson, the switch back to the city (even though a small one) created leisure time problems. One expects to find things provided — commercial amusements — but activities for teenagers seemed to be extremely limited. There were movies twice a week, a few of which we all attended, but it was obvious that the young folks who flocked to the community hall (which doubled as a theater) were more interested in talking and fooling around noisily than they were in watching the picture. It seemed more like a Saturday afternoon children's matinee back home in California. There was an ice-skating rink open for a few hours some evenings, but basically the use of the rink was preempted for hockey practice and games. The most popular gathering place seemed to be one of the local cafes with its blaring juke-box — a typical youthful preference for just hanging around.

All that school year Larry had attempted to reach young people of the community by directing badminton and ping-pong sessions for different age groups several nights a week in the school gymnasium. This was rather successful except that the same eager-beaver kids came each time. He was happy that these youngsters were enjoying some good clean fun, but the ones he was hoping to reach were just not interested.

At the end of January it was time to say good-bye to Larry and head back to Manson. We asked Lyn if she'd like to go back with us, and to our surprise she didn't rebel and was actually willing to go. She had done well in school, made several good friends, but was missing the familiar warmth of a real home atmosphere to come home to. She finished the year by correspondence, but not with the Government courses. The Principal of the Fort St. James school allowed her to take the textbooks to Manson, and the teachers mailed all the assignments which she completed at home and sent back. By June she had done the work so well that it was not required for her to write examinations. She took one trip back to the Fort anyway, to see her friends and to help Larry clean out the apartment and make the move back home to Manson Creek.

This year of Lyn's being involved with the Public School program was certainly an eye-opener to me. The amount of work required to be done was smaller by far than for the B.C. Correspondence School. The same material is covered by both school systems each year, but a safe estimate would be that the Government courses require four or five (or maybe more) times the quantity of written work and reading.

Since the first year with them we had been writing letters and gently trying to point out to the government school some of our observations and thoughts on improvements, but naturally nothing was accomplished. Every so often the kids would get discouraged and we'd make every effort to arouse some enthusiasm, trying not to let them see that we were totally in agreement with their distress. Our letters to the school in those earlier years were strictly between us (Larry and myself) and the directors of the schools. Their replies were sincere, but it was pointed out that for many years the schools had served thousands of students by mail, that the courses had been highly praised, and that while some up-dating might be in order, still budgets were low and there was not much could be done at the present time. We continued writing letters since we felt we were more right than they were.

During this period while Larry was away from us in Fort St. James, a beautiful relationship developed at home between the girls and me.

110

Never had there been so much close togetherness. Each night after Bob and Carolyn had retired to their cabin, and we'd gotten Evy to bed and turned off the generator, we'd sit around the fire talking until the wee hours. Ordinarily lights-out would mean going-to-bed time, but we gradually eased into the habit of sitting in the darkened cosy room and drifting into all sorts of topics of conversation. It wasn't long before we were into the more delicate aspects of boy-girl relationships, as well as marriage and all its involvements. The girls were sixteen and fourteen then and of course the time was right for some mother-daughter plain talk. Inevitably, we arrived at the delightful phase of the sessions in which the girls were thinking up topics and questions to fire at me each night. That lights-out discussion time became very precious to all of us. I could heartily recommend it to all families. Sadly, though, few people are in a position to be able to sit up late every night. They are restricted by the demands on early morning hours of each next day.

During this time the girls also began perfecting their skills in all the domestic arts. For a while we were deluged with quantities of beautiful baked goodies.

Together we viewed our indoor surroundings with a critical eye and decided that some changes were in order. Since the Owen house was more or less the social center of Manson Creek it should be a little more presentable than it was. We perused magazines and catalogues for ideas and were delighted with the final effect when we put it all together.

The paint job came first — a very light beige colour on walls and ceiling to complement the dark brick-red asbestos tile flooring. A long sofa (or Chesterfield) and two big arm-chairs of soft black leather replaced the atrocious odds and ends of furniture we'd been living with. An over-sized dinette set, bronze and beige coloured, graced the dining area in place of the home-made wooden table and odd assorted chairs. Dark brown curtains set off the very bright east window area, and as a finishing touch, jade-green and turquoise bits of colour here and there brightened the scene. The total effect was slightly Spanish, which may seem incongruous for the Canadian bush, but it was cool and pleasant in summer, and warm and friendly in winter.

After school was over in June, Larry returned to take up where he had left off the previous September. Robert and Carolyn stayed on until the end of summer, at which time Larry went with them as far as Prince George to attend to the legal details of the partnership separation, and then to bid them adieu.

Now we were on our own. It was a pleasant, free feeling, but we still had to admit that way back in the beginning we never would have started out to Canada alone. In the four summers and three winters of our togetherness, Larry had learned a great deal from Robert by way of mechanical and technical projects. Carolyn, who was only about five years older than our elder daughter, Lynlee, had been a lively companion and lots of fun for both our girls, as well as a second mother to Evy. We never did feel too much of a generation gap within our family, but Robert and Carolyn were certainly bridges over whatever gap the difference in our ages naturally afforded. We were grateful to them in many ways, and when we said "goodbye" it was with all good wishes for much happiness and contentment to come their way.

Education in the Bush 24

When Lynlee had re-applied for her correspondence school work after the year in public school, and the two girls resumed their lessons, discouragement set in very rapidly. In fact, Lyn was disheartened at the very first assignment. The amount of reading and written work required for each subject in ninth to twelfth grades was staggering, and reminded me vividly of the work hours I used to spend on university subjects. This is no exaggeration. We were honestly appalled at the number of hours our girls had to spend in order to accomplish one day's work in each of their seven or eight subjects.

"Literature" was Leslee's favourite, and even those books were in danger of being tossed into the creek at one point. She had been assigned to read Thor Hyerdal's "Kon-Tiki Expedition" which she did with great enjoyment. The reading was thoroughly pleasurable, but the pages and pages of questions which accompanied each day's work seemed unnecessary. Besides this daily probing behind the scenes, there was another complete series of questions to be answered when the book was finished.

In a classroom it's fun and interesting to analyze stories and poems. Twenty or thirty students expressing opinions promotes a cross-fertilization of ideas which is stimulating and productive. But for one student alone to try to pick the story to pieces, wondering what the author might have had in mind at this point and that, seems almost completely futile. This particular lack is one we were aware of, and was actually our responsibility since we had subjected our children to this remote experience. But even so, for the school to expect any one child working alone to work up enthusiasm for the impossible seemed rather unrealistic.

It was at this point that I wrote another letter to the school headquarters in Leslee's behalf. In reply they granted her the privilege of skipping "Practise Exercises" in certain subjects on condition that her grades in the "Exercise Sections" remain at their very excellent level. It was one small victory and a baby-step in the right direction. But it wasn't just for our kids that I was looking for favours. I was after a bigger change in total policy.

The correspondence school program was set up originally to serve children living in very remote areas — farms, lighthouse stations, etc. — which were too distant from any public school; but over the years it has expanded to include children hospitalized on a long-term basis, children traveling with their parents and living abroad, and young people and adults confined in prisons or correctional institutions.

The twelve grades are divided into Elementary (first through seventh) and General Secondary (eighth through twelfth). At present there may be a thousand students in the elementary grades, and most of them are doing their entire year's schooling by this means. But of the perhaps twenty thousand enrolled in the high school grades, very few are doing their complete schooling by correspondence. Many of these enrollees are actually public school students who are picking up one course which they might not be able to take in their public school. Many are adults who wish to enrich their lives by taking a class or two of further education.

Each High School course has been designed as a thorough and complete year's work, and is divided into eighteen or twenty two-week lessons. There are "Practise Exercises" each day which the student writes out after he has read and absorbed the material. He corrects this work each day from the answer section which is also provided at the back of the workbook. At the end of the two-week lesson there is the "Exercise Section" (without answers in the back) which must be completed in writing, removed from the book, and sent in for grading.

This may not seem so devastating to the casual observer, but when the student has to read and absorb the material entirely on his own, there is a vast difference from what is required of the public school pupil who sits in his class and listens to the teacher explain the background and lead-up material for the day's work to be done. With diligence, one can incorporate one or two courses into a daily routine and get them completed in the allotted time; but seven or eight subjects per day for the student doing all his schooling by correspondence is too much to expect from anyone. By the time most rural students have struggled through eight or nine grades, they usually find a way to move out to a city and go to public school, or else they just drop out completely.

The directors of the school will admit that the drop-out rate is discouragingly high, yet they take no means to improve the situation. The solving of this dilemna seems so simple that I fail to see why they

114

cannot make some radical changes. For instance, each course could be divided into two quantities of required work: (1) Leave everything just as it is for the student taking only one or two subjects; but (2) trim each course down to bare bones for students doing their entire schooling by correspondence.

It's possible for an adult who dropped out of school as a youth, and desires later to get his diploma, to go to night school and complete several years of work in only a matter of several months. If only the directors and teachers who make up the lessons could realize that children and young people living anywhere under remote conditions are experiencing an education — even without books and formal classes — which most school children could never duplicate or even imagine.

Even though we were all unhappy with the only method of schooling which was available to us, still Larry and I felt that we had done the right thing in making this move to the North. The girls were both progressing nicely in every other way. They were avid book-readers and perused news magazines, thereby keeping up with world events generally. They could both express themselves well in writing, be it a school composition or a letter to a friend. They taught themselves to use the typewriter and became adequately proficient. They both appreciated and preferred classical music records, but occasionally our ear drums would be battered by the radio sounds of popular music at the teenage level. We were pleased with the ease and ability both our daughters displayed in meeting and conversing with adults and all the new people they'd meet each time they took their turn behind the counter in the store.

They became adept in the kitchen and household arts, and in addition learned to drive the truck a few years before they were old enough to be legally licensed. They could fish; they could help disembowel a moose and butcher the meat. They could discuss geology in a little more than a beginner's style, and could produce a beautiful and perfect ring stone from a slab of rock.

Life here was one big learning experience for all of us, and the only heartache was to see the girls bogged down with such a heavy load of schoolwork. We compared notes often with the Westfalls and the Jacks at Germansen, and later on with others who moved into the area. Everyone's opinion mirrored ours. We've all written imploring and explaining letters through the years and will continue to do so. Perhaps some day our ideas may bear fruit.

Digging a Grave   25

Our senior oldtimer, Bob Watson, was getting along in years and had developed diabetes. He was needing daily medical attention, so on doctor's orders he moved from Manson out to Fort St. James. Within a year's time we received word that he had died in hospital. Since he was far removed from any relatives, and since Manson was the only home he'd known for forty years, we all agreed that he should be brought back here for burial. At a time of death, a day or two can make a lot of difference and since we hadn't received the message immediately, other plans were already underway and a grave had been prepared for him out in the city. There was a bit of a hassle to make changes at this late date, but with the understanding help of friends in the Fort St. James branch of the Canadian Legion, of which Bob had been a member, the change in arrangements was accomplished.

Then we were faced with a job we'd never done before: digging a grave. We scrutinized our little rail-fenced burial ground with new intent. There were two rows of grave plots and only six burials that anyone could be sure of. Some were marked by homemade wooden crosses with nail-studded lettering. Some were not marked at all. The earliest had been in 1940 and the grave was occupied by a man who had died of ptomaine poisoning. Another spot contained the body of a man who'd drowned in Germansen Lake when the "Cat" he'd been operating was backed too far and plunged into an undetermined depth of water. One man had committed suicide with his own rifle, and another had drowned in the creek just outside of town when he fell through thin ice with snowshoes on his feet. A sawmill accident resulted in the death from loss of blood for a man whose arm had been cut off.

The latest burial had occurred the year before we came to Canada. One of the slightly eccentric oldtimers was very ill but absolutely refused medical treatment. He died the way he preferred — in his sleep and in his own cabin. But during the arrangements for his burial a feud developed between two of the neighbors which hasn't been resolved to this day, and probably never will be. One friend had designed and built a fine casket before he knew that the intended occupant had stiffened into something other than the conventional burial position. The only thing the others could think of to do was to rebuild the coffin the accommodate the position of the deceased. But the first man who applied the pry-bar to begin the dismantling of this lovely piece of furniture became the object of a ten years' silent feud with the original builder.

I'm a firm believer in the adage that "man was not meant to live alone," and it's been my observation that the ones who do tend toward a slight deviation from the norm. I'm certainly not suggesting that extremes of odd behaviour or attitude are always the case. Usually the evidence of a hard-headed, unrelenting attitude is most obvious in little things that don't really matter.

But back to the graveyard . . . The old-timers remembered all the people they had buried, but were in some confusion over which plots were unoccupied. On their general agreement that the northeast corner should be empty, that's where we started digging. The young boys from Germansen had come over for the day, and in a gesture of friendship, they did most of the pick and shovel work. It happened to be a hot, sultry day so Lyn and Les kept the cookies, lemonade, and conversation flowing. Only when the diggers had reached the six-foot level without running into any dull thuds of white bones did we know for sure that we had chosen a safe spot.

When the hole was completed, tape measures were applied to be sure of the proper depth and dimensions. Everyone was listening and shuddering as Jack Thomson told of one of the burials one winter when the ground was so frozen and digging such an effort that they all agreed it would be alright to stop at three or four feet down. Next spring when the ground thawed and the wind blew across town from that certain direction, the fragrance was almost unbearable. No one relished the idea of a repetition of that experience.

In early evening of the following day, while the sun was still high in the western sky, our freighter arrived in his big red truck with its customary load of gas, groceries, and mail; but this time he also had the casket containing the body of our old friend, Bob. All the local population, plus friends from Germansen, and even a few interested summer visitors, had gathered in front of the store to join together for the simple unceremonious goodbye.

When the flag-draped coffin had been removed from the truck, the procession of friends made its way from the road onto a little path which led behind a cabin, past a woodshed, through the trees, and on to the small cemetery. Bob's friends had been of all ages, so the pall bearers picked at random were four older men and two nineteen-year-olds.

Bruce Russell had volunteered to lead the brief service, and mentioned that he had driven Bob up into this area when he first came out from the East in the "hungry thirties." The twenty-five people assembled stood around casually in small groups, or leaned back against the rail fence. Several recalled experiences with Bob and shared them informally with the gathering. Overt sadness was not evident. Bob had lived a good and busy life, had died at age eighty-five, and had already become almost legendary among the individual placer miners of this part of the country.

When the coffin was being lowered, one corner of it caught on a small protruding shelf of earth. It was brought up again and one of the boys jumped down into the hole with a pick to remove the offending area, and then the proceedings continued. Anywhere else such a breach in solemn proceedings would be gauche. Here it didn't matter at all. Each of Bob's friends threw a few shovelfuls of earth back into the grave. Everyone stayed until the job was completed and the new mound covered with a huge wreath which our girls and their friends had created from pine boughs and wild flowers, shaped and wired together.

Although I've been to many fine funerals in beautiful chapels and well-tended cemeteries, none has ever impressed me as much as did the natural surroundings and beautiful simplicity of that ceremony.

The Kids are Growing up 26

Time was passing and our family was maturing. Evy, who had been a toddler when we first came to Canada, had graduated into a new stage of development known as the helpful age. He was the only child in our area, so was accepted into most every situation and activity. Had there been even two youngsters around, they would have been considered a nuisance during work times and told to run away and play. But since Evy was just one small body and one set of busy hands to watch, he was a part of all the building, repairing, wood-cutting, and recreational activities that went on in his all-adult world.

The first couple of years I used to wonder about the wisdom of allowing our small child to grow up in this situation where there were no others his age around for so much of the time. I needn't have worried, however. To our surprise, whenever there were playmates, he happily and readily shared toys, pets, food, and just anything that the other child might want. There had been no teaching or learning program along this line, he just seemed to be generous by nature. A psychologist would probably have some explanation on this point, but I certainly couldn't understand it since children are supposed to be basically selfish until they are taught otherwise.

Ev was a friendly little fellow and readily made the acquaintance of anyone working or mining in the vicinity. He was always watching machinery at work, and proudly rode in the cab of almost every piece of heavy equipment that came into the area. Our truck motor never once started up without our young one dropping whatever he was doing and making a dash for his place in the back. No one ever started out for a hike in summer or a snowshoe walk in winter without Evy going along, too. He was ever -present and was somehow accepted without rancor. For him the supreme punishment was not to be allowed to go along when someone was going somewhere. This would happen only rarely.

One day when Larry and Ev were on the way to Germansen Landing, it was their unfortunate luck to have the truck develop a problem more serious than Larry could analyze or repair. All that was left to do was to start walking the nine miles back home. Inconceivably, for the time of year, no vehicles happened along, so they made the entire trip back on foot. Evy came running into the house and had the whole episode related before his dad had even reached the front porch. Next moment our small whirlwind was outside wielding a badminton racquet and exhibiting the energy of one who might have just arisen from a refreshing nap. Larry collapsed on the couch.

I'd hate to admit the tender age at which Ev was handling an axe. The first time was terrifying. He brought in a small bundle of kindling which he'd cut, unsupervised. We immediately laid down rules and regulations involving use of the axe. But on the day that he unloaded and stacked a truckbed full of wood which the men had just brought in, we began to take more realistic stock of his ability. The men had taken time out for coffee before unloading and making another trip, and Evy had thrown all the wood off the truck into the woodshed and had almost finished stacking it before we even knew what he was up to. Most children his age are not allowed near the woodpile, except to fetch a load for the stove. We decided that perhaps he was ready for a bit more responsibility, so after that Larry would take him along on woodcutting trips and let him limb-off branches from the trees which had been felled. Evy was in such a hurry to do grownup things.

When nothing else was going on, however, he would retire to his favourite digging spot across the road from Johnny's cabin. The dirt was soft and sandy there, and every summer day for four or five years, Ev would spend happy hours in his pit. One day there would be an intricate network of roads for his fleet of toy cars and trucks. Another day his small models of earth-moving machinery would keep the boundaries of the pit ever changing. One child alone could play there happily for hours, and when he had young guests to entertain, they also were invited to share the joys of the pit.

Evy had observed enough cribbage-playing in Johnny's cabin that by the time he had learned to count and do some elemental adding and subtracting, he was sitting up at the crib table and playing his cards like a small sized "pro". During the early years of his playing he was dealt the almost impossible "29-hand". It was a legitimate deal. No one was doing him any favours. He knew that he'd hit the jackpot, but what he wasn't aware of was just how infrequently this happens. Johnny, who has been playing for years and years, has never been so blessed, so in honour of the occasion he presented Evy with one of the trophies from his shelf which read, "World's Greatest Card Player". The other player who had dealt the hand sent in a small article to the Fort St. James newspaper.

A few years more and he could repair his own bicycle, patch his bike tires, and even assist in the repairing of automobile tires. He knew where tools were kept, which tools were needed for which job, and how to use them. When adults would comment on his adeptness and eagerness he appeared to pay no attention to their praise, but if it did sink in, it only served to double his zeal.

During times when no other children were around he was a contented and worthwhile helper around town and in the store; but with the appearance of one more child, he would magically turn into an average, normal kid and suddenly was nowhere to be found when a job needed doing.

*   *   *   *   *   *

Our daughters had reached their mid-teen years and had definitely become interested in the world of the opposite sex. Whenever a car drove up and stopped at the store, its occupants were given a casual scrutiny from our house windows. If anyone of interest had appeared, the girls willingly volunteered to do store duty. Sometimes one would go, sometimes the other, and occasionally both together for moral support. But if Lyn was at the store and had been gone too long, Leslee would invariably find an excuse to go over there, too. I'm sure that many of our visitors were surprised to find these youthful and charming store proprietors in such an out-of-the-way place.

Since this area where we live is, of course, predominantly a man's environment, the girls naturally and happily met many young men. There was a decided dearth of girl friends, but this only served to draw the sisters closer together. Leslee, the younger, caught up and surpassed Lynlee in height, so the girls for a while were taken for twins, and later Leslee was even thought to be the older, much to Lyn's dismay.

Our daughters were well aware of the fact that mining companies who bring prospecting teams into the area each summer usually hire college geology students, so each season's new "crop" was awaited and speculated upon. Evidently the situation worked in reverse also, because a few years later we were told of a conversation between one of our oldtimers and some young men who had stopped on the road about forty miles before reaching Manson. They were drinking coffee by a campfire, and when they found the older man was a resident of Manson Creek they inquired if what they had heard was true: that there were a couple of beautiful girls at Manson. We laughed over that one. So much more was implied than was the case. Lyn and Les were just two happy and enthusiastic young kids.

One day a Vancouver supervisor of one of the mining companies drove up to Manson to check out his men, and found one of them in our kitchen busily stirring up a birthday cake for Leslee. Since it was a Sunday and not a workday, there were no difficulties this time — only surprised reactions on both sides. But when the same supervisor came up again a month later and found the same young man playing volleyball in our yard with about six other kids, and it didn't happen to be his day off, young Paul was a bit more embarrassed. Actually he had come into town to buy some groceries for the camp and had merely taken a little time out to join the game which was in progress. The boss was a lively sort himself, however, and since Paul was one of the company's ace prospectors, he got by with only a mild reprimand and a reminder of his duty to the company.

*   *   *   *   *   *

The day that Lyn and Les got their first helicopter ride was the biggest thrill in their thus-far lives. A pilot had stopped in unexpectedly, wanting to use our radio-phone, but that day the radio-reception was too weak.

"I'll have to hop over to Germansen and try there," he said. "You young ladies want to come with me? I'll have you back in half an hour."

The girls were speechless, but we had to urge them only a moment and they were eagerly dashing under the whirling blades to take their places and be strapped in on either side of the pilot.

As they lifted off, Larry commented, "Won't this be something to write home about!" Slightly in awe of the whole thing, and of a more practical bent, I wondered if we'd see them alive again. But since those early days we came to realize that planes and helicopters are very much a part of the development in the north country, and through the years we've all had many rides in both types of aircraft.

*   *   *   *   *   *

It wasn't too many years before we began considering our house too small for our growing-up family. We talked of pushing out a wall, opening up the attic, making the back room into a bedroom, but nothing developed until Lyn got the bright idea of moving herself into the little rental cabin next door. It was a brilliant solution. The cabin sat only about twenty feet apart from our house, so it was almost an extension anyway. Lyn moved her clothes and possessions, her paints and easel,

122

and all of her other artistic projects, and set up housekeeping next door. For a while she would fix breakfast and lunch for herself and would eat dinner with us. But since she never did really get excited about cooking for one, or even for keeping her few dishes washed up, the novelty soon wore off. Lyn wasn't really a housekeeper. Her temperament was definitely artistic. She did enjoy having the space to stretch out in, however, and enjoyed a bit of privacy for a change. It didn't bother us a bit that she bounced back home to do her eating.

*　　*　　*　　*　　*　　*

With our population as sparse as it is, when people go visiting they go as a family, and we return visits the same way. It took me a while to get used to this because in our former urban living situation I had most thoroughly enjoyed the evenings out when all children had been left behind with babysitters. Back there it seemed that about the only times people would go anywhere as a family were to church once a week, or for a summer holiday trip once a year. Things are done differently in the northern bush, however. The kids grow up knowing adults on a first-name basis. They are never shooed out of adult conversations, and have become an all-day, every-day, ever-present part of the life. I can't remember many times when anything that happened was purposely kept from the children's ears. Good news, bad news, happiness or tragedy were all shared by everyone. With no television screens to monopolize our time and interfere with visiting, we rediscovered the fine art of conversation. Of course when the kids would tire of adult chatter they'd drift outside to play ball or badminton, sit on the porch swing and talk, go for walks, visit the beaver house, throw rocks in the creek, or do most anything they could think up to do.

But it wasn't just with the local residents that we hobnobbed. Our lives were enriched in unusual ways by people from the outside world whom we met and spent time with. The family, of course, shared in these learning sessions.

For part of a week we had a rather successful American author staying with us. He was gathering book material and was traveling extensively in northern British Columbia, staying long enough in many of the small towns to talk with the old-timers as well as the new-comers. It was with special interest that we read the newly published book later on, and also saw his picture along with the book review in TIME and NEWSWEEK magazines.

Another summer we met a vitally interesting young couple — he, an entomologist and she, a geologist — both instructors in an Alberta University. Their trip into our area was primarily in her behalf, but he brought along his nets and bottles and paraphernalia for collecting insects, while his wife was looking over rock and mineral formations. Lyn and Les were intrigued with the "bug man" and it wasn't long before they were engaged in helping to look for specimens of creepy, crawly things. The girls were so cooperative that he left a rack of small bottles containing formaldehyde, and gave them instructions on how to collect and preserve spiders. At the end of summer they could package up the bottles and send them to him. He was doing a graduate paper on the subject and needed specimens for illustrations.

The girls set to work with glee. Every time they went walking, a jar went along with them. I was horrified at some of the winners they came up with — some hairy, some sleek, some bulbously fat, some with eggs on their backs — all in all a gruesome display to anyone like me who doesn't appreciate the world of spiders.

But the entomologist loved them! Shortly after receiving the package he sent the girls an enthusiastic letter.

"Dear Lyn and Les,

Your package of spiders arrived yesterday, and I spent the evening poring over them. There is one, an *Amaurobiidea*, that is really good. It was a male, and I have no males in my collection, so this is the first one I've seen. He is the pale-coloured spider with the yellow and brown streaks on the abdomen, and is about the same size as the wolf spiders you got. He was probably caught under a stone near a grassy area? That is where I have collected the females. Many thanks for this real prize!"

*　　*　　*　　*　　*　　*

On a different occasion a casual conversation with new friends revealed that they owned a tree farm in Ontario. None of us had ever even heard of a tree farm, but learned that it is exactly what the name implies: a tree-covered area which is managed as a business enterprise, with the owners personally handling or contracting for all the work involved in the management — logging, clearing, abatement of hazards, re-planting, etc.

This couple explained their work and showed us how to tell the age of a standing pine tree by the number of layers of branches. The varying height of space between layers indicates the good, average, or poor years of growth. The taller the space, the better the growing season that particular year.

There was another couple interested in trees, but their line of endeavor took a different approach. They lived in our area for a few years and made a thriving little business of carving and polishing tree burls. A burl is actually part of the tree trunk, an abnormal protrusion

124

which was caused sometime in the early stages of the tree's development. Some burls will be about the size of a fist, while others could be as large as three feet in diameter.

Frank and Lois Woodford began working with these burls after they moved into the Manson-Germansen area. Frank had been an assistant to a hunting guide, and they had come each year from their home in Alberta. When Frank retired they decided to live for a while in a cabin at Germansen Lake. It was there that they began this new project. They'd go out with the chainsaw and cut off the burls parallel to the tree trunk. After harvesting a crop, the real work began at home. First the bark is peeled off, the inside is carved out, and they are set to dry for a time. After extensive sanding, and a coat or two of varnish, the finished product is a lovely wooden bowl. From the larger burls Frank has sawn off "slices" and made bread-boards, carving boards, and even small table tops. Variation in finished products is dependent only on one's versatility and imagination.

For a couple of winters Lyn, Les, and even Evy spent part of their leisure hours working along with Frank and Lois in the fashioning of these beautiful products.

*   *   *   *   *   *

We all had a pleasurable learning experience when our neighbor, Johnny, invited his teenage granddaughter, June, to come for a visit from her home in Denmark. She arrived with a girl friend, Brigitta ("Gitty" for short). They stayed about six weeks and proved to be a lively twosome. It was fun to have a couple more girls around for a change, and for the Danish visitors as well as for ourselves, the comparing of ideas was educational and interesting. The girls had learned English in school, but this was their first attempt at conversational English on this side of the world. Gitty, being the lively one of the two, took the lead in expressing thoughts and ideas for both of them, but whenever she was stumped for the right word, June provided it even before Gitty could turn to her for the assistance.

June came back each summer for several years and each time vowed that someday she was going to live in the Canadian North!

*   *   *   *   *   *

We've become acquainted with college professors, school teachers, and principals who, like everyone else, would be making a trip into our area either for a family outing, a hunting trip, or just for a one-day excursion to see what was at the other end of the long north road. The fact of their profession would be revealed in one way or another as soon as they discovered there were children and young people here, and no evidence of a school building. People in the field of education are always curious and questioning. (I suppose it is either a natural pre-requisite for an interest in education in the first place, or else it's a natural result of the profession.) But invariably we'd be engaged in conversation for at least an hour while they'd inquire about the way of our lives here and how the formal schooling is handled and how we like it.

$$* \quad * \quad * \quad * \quad * \quad *$$

After Lyn and Les reached the so-called "dating age" they were seldom without male companions, but this was nothing new because a predominance of men was exactly what they'd grown up with here at Manson. We were aware that the young men were coming to visit a little more often, and our home was turning into an ever more popular spot. For a few years Keith and Doug from Germansen were frequently around. They knew that they were always welcome — mealtime and anytime. Actually there was a vast age range in the young friends who frequented our home — all the way from sixteen to thirty — but with all of them, the most indulged-in pastime was sitting around the kitchen table joking, laughing and talking. Occasionally one of them would be recruited to ice a cake or peel apples for a pie. Complete informality prevailed at all times. And I guess Larry and I must have been considered acceptable company because all the visitors seemed completely content and happy to sit and talk with all of us. That horribly-feared generation-gap just didn't seem to exist, and we parents had the rare privilege of getting to know our daughters' friends almost as well as the girls did themselves.

The kids weren't totally sedentary, however. Their youthful enthusiasm found many outlets. During the hottest part of summer there was a lot of swimming at nearby little Slate Lake. The lakes in the area are never really warm, but Slate Lake being the shallowest naturally becomes the warmest; so when the summer temperature climbed to ninety degrees, that water was mighty inviting. Bonfires were always a delightful accompaniment to a swimming party, and frequently wiener or marshmallow roasts were included. Leslee learned to play guitar and had many and varied instructors along the way. Amazing how much guitar-playing went on in the house and around campfires.

Our daughters matured rapidly, but depending on the age and mood of their current associates, they could act very juvenile or extremely grown-up. The same applied to the men. On occasion thirty-year-olds have been seen playing hop-scotch in the dirt road out front.

126

I often thought of Manson Creek as a melting pot of age groups. Our children grew up accustomed to dealing with people of all ages, with some much older, with some of their parents' ages, and with some who were young like themselves. It all helped to make life run more smoothly.

Problems Medical 27

With all this good life, one might get the impression that nothing disappointing, frustrating, or terrifying ever happens in the north country. Things are no different here than anywhere else in the world where human inter-relationships are involved. The difference in environment, however, does often provide a unique intrigue to problems.

We are asked repeatedly by tourists how we handle emergencies; more particularly, what we do when we need a doctor. Answering this question and watching reactions, I have observed that people differ amazingly in their attitudes toward sickness, accidents, and the assurance of nearby medical assistance. And the range of attitude runs all the way from the super hypochondriac who would rush to the doctor with a sneeze, to the hermit who prefers to live and die in his cave (or cabin) far removed from civilization. Our own personal position would be somewhere along the halfway mark on the scale, with a slight inclination toward the hermit's direction. It has never been our habit to bother doctors unnecessarily with minor complaints, and fortunately we've all enjoyed rather excellent health. At the same time, however, we've always had tremendous respect for the medical profession.

Back in California when we were contemplating this move into the northern bush country, we discussed the handling of medical problems in the same vein as we did food problems, living problems, school problems, and all the rest. It was assumed, quite logically, that there probably wouldn't be any contagious diseases to worry about in this colder, isolated climate, but we still put together a generously stocked medical kit which included any antibiotics the doctor could give us. We felt that Larry's reasonably adequate first-aid knowledge would suffice in case of more serious accidents, until licensed medical help could be summoned. Thus armed, we ventured forth unafraid.

Through the years here we've seen our share of accidents, and have been instrumental in either treating them ourselves or in phoning out for emergency aid by air. For the wintry half of the year those are the only two choices for the injured. The rest of the time when the road is open and driveable, there is the added option of journeying to a doctor or hospital by car or truck. Many family injuries which we ourselves successfully treated were of a serious enough nature that I know we would have rushed to a doctor had we been living in the city. And I know just as surely that if we ever move back to "civilization", we'll not think twice about going to a doctor with an injury; we'll just go, like everyone else does. But nowhere is the adage about necessity being the mother of invention more applicable than 120 miles from the nearest hospital. As it turned out, only one member of our family had to be flown out for medical reasons and, ironically, the incident happened after nine years of serious-accident-free living in the North. Lynlee fell off a runaway horse and dislocated her shoulder.

Since our home was the headquarters of the small settlement, some exciting scares and worries have been brought to our doorstep for attention. One of the old Indian men, living alone at the lake, was doing a filthy and inadequate first-aid job to his own foot which, unknown to anyone else, had been deeply and seriously cut by an old rusty length of metal stovepipe. When a friend stopped by one day to say hello, he found the stoical old man casually carving some of the almost gangrenous flesh away from the week-old wound. We phoned for a plane to take him out promptly! There have been a few cases of crushed hands or fingers where men have been involved with heavy mining and earth-moving machinery. The axe-cuts to hands, legs and feet have been too numerous to mention, and have varied in severity. During a tourist family's fishing outing, one of their little girls was standing in the wrong spot and caught a fish-hook deeply into her forearm. In another instance, a small boy had the last inch of his middle finger half severed during some unsupervised play.

There was only one case of appendicitis, and the young man safely and in time made it out to the hospital by road; but again we phoned for a plane in a hurry when we were confronted with a case of blood poisoning. It was the first I'd ever seen, and sure enough, the tell-tale red streak of the medical guide books was plainly visible up the fellow's arm.

We haven't been called on to deliver any babies, but Wes at Germansen has. A full-term pregnant Indian woman was being flown out from farther up north, and the plane was forced down by bad weather. The pilot and passengers had to overnight in cabins at Germansen Landing. The imminent arrival wasn't interested in waiting, however, and Wes and Maggie assisted at the birth. The new baby boy was named after his "doctor" in gratitude.

There have been several unexpected deaths, each of which created its own flurry of activity. One old prospector was found dead on the road about fifty miles west of Manson. He was too old to have been out there alone, but old prospectors are a breed all their own. He'd presumably had problems with the truck so had started walking for help. He'd lain down by the side of the road to rest, fallen asleep, and never awakened. Two startled hunters happened upon his body.

A husky, young, experienced cowhand, traveling with a party of hunters, was swept off his horse by the fast-moving current of the river he was crossing. His body was never recovered.

For as far back as any of the residents can remember, there has been but one fatal traffic accident on "our road", and this happened during the decade we lived there. One passenger died instantly in the collision, and the other who seemed unhurt at the time, collapsed and died that evening at home. These were two members of the Indian family living at Wolverine Lake.

We thought that our sixteen-year-old Leslee was going to suffer a very personal emotional tragedy when we heard a radio news report that two people had been killed in a plane accident. The report came in on the 9:00 p.m. news and stated that a small plane with two people aboard had crashed and burned in the remote northern settlement of Germansen Landing, killing both passengers!

Les was positive that Keith Westfall, the object of her young love, who was taking flying lessons with his dad, had failed on a landing or takeoff and was now lying dead in a mass of burning wreckage. I must admit we all felt that the odds lay in that direction since the brief description of the aircraft sounded like Westfall's plane. There isn't all that much air traffic at Germansen, usually, and six o'clock in the evening (twilight time in September) is an uncommon hour for anyone from the outside to be either arriving or departing. We figured the victims surely had to be either Wes and Keith, or Wes and Maggie, or Wes and someone. All of us were shaken to the core since this terrible thing was happening to our very good friends. The previous winter we had come to know Keith like our own because every second or third week he'd snowshoe over to spend a weekend with us, and especially to see Leslee.

For an hour we kept switching the radio to different stations hoping to pick up more details and names, but while the report was on every news broadcast, no further information was given. Our radio-phone never did work after dark, so we were thwarted there. Finally Larry could stand it no longer. He and I decided to take a run over to Germansen to see what help and consolation could be offered. It wasn't until we were almost there that we suddenly realized the accident might possibly have happened at Gene Jack's airstrip, and to a plane belonging to someone altogether unknown to us. All our thinking heretofore had been centered around the old picturesque truss bridge across the river which has often been considered hazardous to air traffic landing or taking off on the river.

When we reached Gene's camp, sure enough, we could just discern the jagged and crumpled outline of a plane at the edge of the runway near the road. Small wisps of smoke were still rising from the wreckage.

Gene's son, Doug, was alone at the camp that night, and he had been officially put in charge of keeping any onlookers away until the next morning when Department of Transport officials could get in and take over. Doug came out when he saw our car's headlights, and answered our first urgent question, telling us that the victims were a married couple from another town who had just stopped by to let off a passenger — a mechanic who was going to work in the area. The crash had occurred as they were taking off again.

Doug insisted that we come in for a bit before heading back home. He put on a pot of coffee while he and the shaken mechanic told us more of the details, and still tried to figure in their own minds what could have caused the crash.

As it happened, we did know the victims. They'd rented a cabin from us at Manson earlier that same summer. We told Doug about Leslee's frantic reaction, and he said that he'd tell Keith to get over to Manson in the morning and present himself alive and well.

A plane crash anywhere causes a lot of commotion, and things were really active up in our part of the country the next day. There were planes and helicopters overhead, R.C.M.P. men by car over the road, and several small congregations of tourists who were driving by during the day and were in awe of the horror of the happening. Don Gilliland (from Germansen) stopped by for coffee later on, on his way out to Prince George. Upon further questioning, he quietly admitted that he had been commissioned to drive the two bodies out to the morgue. I shuddered momentarily to think that in the back of that truck outside were two charred human bodies enclosed in plastic bags; and not too long ago those same two bodies, alive and well, had been visitors to our town and had stayed with us a while. Life is indeed uncertain!

* * * * * *

The death by illness and exposure of one of our young friends resulted in an intriguing revelation of past history. Sam was almost thirty years old when we first met him, and it wasn't until he returned the second year that we realized he meant to become one of the "regulars" in our part of the country. Sam wasn't much more than five and a half feet tall, and weighed a mere 130 pounds. He was in the habit of stopping in to visit often and was a lively conversationalist. He seemed well indoctrinated in mining and mineralogy, and the stories he told indicated that he'd done a lot of moving around between the extremes of Central America and Alaska. Only occasionally would we glean a slight inkling that he might have done some of that travel in an armchair and with a book. But Sam was good company, and while neither Lyn nor Les was particularly attracted to him, they were friendly; and Sam enjoyed sitting on the sidelines watching their cavortings and taking part in the round-table fun and joking.

The third year of our acquaintanceship Sam had decided that he was going to spend the winter in a cabin about fifty miles north of us, working for one of the trappers up there. He made extensive plans, got in an adequate grub supply, and made arrangements with a friend at Germansen to fly over his camp on the last day of each month to be sure that smoke was coming out the chimney and all was well. But all didn't turn out well. Sam was found dead on the trail at the end of February when his friend instigated a search because there was no sign of life at the camp. The autopsy revealed that Sam had been suffering from a rare wasting disease which he perhaps wasn't even aware of himself. But with absolutely no physical reserve to fall back on during the rigors of winter, and with possibly a serious imbalance of nutrition, Sam in his weakened condition came to an untimely end.

It took a bit of sleuthing and a few weeks' time for officials to find Sam's next of kin, since he'd never talked much about relatives, or where he'd come from. To the absolute amazement of all of us, it was found that he'd left home in Kansas, pretended suicide by leaving clothes and possessions by a bridge, and disappeared, making his way to Canada to seek a new unencumbered life. Left behind were three small daughters and a wife!

The next summer, Sam's mother and father, who'd never given up hope that he hadn't been drowned those few years ago, made a trip to the Canadian North to meet Sam's friends and retrace as much as possible of his existence since he'd left Kansas. We were pleased to meet them, and over the lunch table we told them what we could of Sam's wanderings, showed them snapshots, and Lyn shared with them some personal souvenirs and writings which Sam had given her.

After continuing to Germansen to meet with the rest of their son's friends, the folks stopped by again on their homeward journey. They were grateful to everyone and felt that now the picture was complete.

Their parting invitation was: "If you ever find yourself down Kansas way, be sure to stop in to see us." I responded that I couldn't really imagine we ever would be since most of our relatives and friends were located on the east and west coast areas of the States.

The reply from Sam's mother was a real truism and one I'll never forget: "Don't be too sure. If anyone had told me a year ago that I'd ever be in northern British Columbia, I'd have laughed in their faces. Our going to Canada seemed as remote as going to Africa; but here we are. We just never really know what the future has in store for us, do we?"

* * * * * *

The radio-phone which we had purchased by the second winter of isolated living became a vital part of our way of life. Each morning we'd take a casual survey of weather conditions outside, phone in the report to the airline office in Prince George, and then leave the machine on for a while to listen to the messages, flight reports, and general chatter that went on within the two-hundred mile radius. Much of the almost-continuous flow of radio messages didn't concern us, but it was fun to listen to anyway, and the voices became as familiar as old friends, although we never did meet many of the owners of the voices. Whenever Germansen, or Manson, or Wolverine Lake was mentioned we'd perk up our ears, and if flights were coming in we'd assist on the radio with reports on present cloud and weather conditions in our immediate area.

The prime need for the radio-phone in a remote area is, of course, assurance in time of need — a type of insurance policy. And never did this "insurance" pay off more gratefully than the afternoon when a neighbor came running up the road, blood-spattered, and yelling for me to get on the phone — quick!

"Ben's in bad trouble . . . he's almost blown a leg off . . . down at the lake!"

Momentarily stunned, but quickly recovering, I snapped on the switch and addressed our contact out in civilization: "Manson Creek calling Prince George! Manson Creek calling Prince George!"

Fortunately it was a good day for radio transmission and the reply came through at once: "This is Prince George. Go ahead, Manson Creek."

"Prince George, we need a plane and doctor as fast as possible. There's been a terrible accident with dynamite and one of our residents may have lost a leg!"

"Roger, Manson Creek, I read that. We'll get the action started immediately. Stay by the phone. I'll need to call you again after I line up the doctor. He'll want more details."

"Thanks, Prince George. I'll be right here .·. . and hurry! Manson Creek over and out."

This major emergency was more complicated by far than the minor first aid experience of any of us who were around. Larry, our "rock" in times of distress, was away in Vancouver at the time, but one young man who had spent a few years in the navy gallantly and readily took charge. He called for an old mattress, a pile of blankets, whatever pain-killing drugs we might have, and lots of clean cloths, bandaging and first-aid supplies. Five other young people volunteered their services, and off they all went on the errand of mercy. The crew managed to get the injured two hundred and thirty pound man into a seldom-used old cabin on the shore of Wolverine Lake where they built a fire to keep him warm while awaiting the aircraft and doctor. Thus began what turned into an all-night vigil.

Before radio reception faded with the early twilight of November days, we had received word that the plane was on its way; but two hours later Wes drove from Germansen with news received on his more powerful set, that the rescue craft had encountered a massive storm front and had been forced to turn back. A helicopter pilot was going to attempt to get the doctor in, so the kids were supposed to pick a landing spot and mark it fore and aft with truck headlights, lamps, and any other available light.

At the scene of action about three of the crew had stayed inside to help with the injured man, and the rest who nearly passed out at sight of the ghastly wound and all the bloody surroundings, had chosen to do the outside chores of chopping wood and running errands back and forth between Manson and the lake. This new directive from Mr. Westfall set them to work with renewed zeal. To keep the inside stove and outside bonfire going, they cut trees and chopped them into firewood as long as daylight lasted. As the hours of evening wore on they began tearing down a couple of old outhouse buildings for fire fodder. Later on when the need became urgent they chopped up benches, tables, shelves and anything available to keep the fires going.

During the course of the waiting Ben's buddy revealed the details of the excursion which was ending in disaster. It seemed that Ben, who had "inherited" a litter of six motherless puppies, foresaw a need for quantities of food during the winter after the pups graduated from the bottle-feeding stage, and decided to amass a quantity of fish in the surest and quickest way possible: by tossing a stick of dynamite into the lake. The explosion stuns the fish in the immediate area, and they float to the top. Easy harvesting. Ben knew this was highly illegal, but he was an experienced dynamite man, and this effort was surely in a compassionate cause. No one was quite sure why the explosion occurred

134

at about the same instant the stick was being tossed, but the next moment Ben was lying unconscious with a gaping hole in his leg, a serious injury to his arm, and all his exposed skin peppered with imbedded bits of rock and glass. (The dynamite stick had been enclosed in a bottle.)

The accident happened about three in the afternoon, and by ten at night we had all resigned ourselves to the depressing fact that no doctor was going to get in. Each hour someone drove from the lake back up to the house to report the patient's condition, to pick up needed items for the injured man and to take back coffee and sandwiches for the rescue team. They always asked the same question: "Any further word about the doctor?" And always they received the same negative reply.

The worst wound had been to Ben's leg where the skin and muscle of the calf had been blown to bits right to the bone. Ben had been gravitating back and forth from complete lucidity to unconsciousness, and from a peaceful acceptance of his excruciating pain, to a wild thrashing and flailing of his arms. During these anxious moments the people trying to hold him quiet so the blood vessels wouldn't spew forth again were tossed across the room like sticks of kindling. Aspirins, 222's, and anything else available for relief of pain were vomited back up immediately. The ill-equipped crew felt helpless in this grave emergency, and there was absolutely nothing to do but watch the patient grow paler and weaker by the hour. After midnight, each hourly report from the scene was that he'd never last the night, and each time I heard the truck on the road, I expected to hear that Ben had expired. Already I was thinking of which plots in the cemetery were available. By four in the morning Ben was hanging onto life by a mere thread.

At 4:30, almost unbelievably, truck sounds from another direction were heard by the rescue team at the lake. We hadn't given a thought to anyone driving in from outside because it was assumed that the road was closed with the growing level of early winter snow. (This was November 17th.) Big sighs of relief filled the air as a doctor and an R.C.M.P. officer drove up in a Jeep after a six-hour struggle on the road. The doctor dashed in to the wounded man and went to work immediately. He couldn't find a pulse since all the blood vessels were quite collapsed, so he made an incision in Ben's ankle to start blood transfusions. In moments Ben's eyelids began to flutter and color was returning to his skin. It was the doctor's opinion that had he been delayed even five more minutes, he would have arrived to treat a dead man.

Next morning when the Air Force Search and Rescue Helicopter arrived to ferry the patient to the hospital, Ben was actually revived enough that he was sitting up on the edge of his makeshift bed!

That was a long, long, never-to-be-forgotten night. Lynlee and the other young people had never been involved in anything remotely related to this type of horror, yet they had found themselves capable of rising to the occasion. If Lyn's friend with the Navy experience was playing doctor, she herself was right in there as his right-hand nurse. It hadn't been necessary for everyone to rush to the scene, and I didn't actually care to, anyway. Someone had to stay by the radio-phone and man the home front. But I was certainly proud of all the young people of our little community that night. Even if the patient had died, I still would have given them equal praise for their valiant, faithful and tireless efforts.

This had been our first major calamity, and knowing now with great realism what *can* happen, it was Leslee who decided to go out to Vancouver the next year and take the first series of the highly acclaimed St. John Ambulance First Aid course. She returned with a "C" ticket in industrial first Aid, and began accumulating a stock of equipment and medications. There hasn't been another so serious accident, but I've been happy to have had Leslee's newly acquired skills available in several lesser emergencies.

Trials and Tribulations 28

For all our years at Manson we lived with the lack of running water in the house. One of my first demands when we decided to settle here was that we just had to rig up some sort of water system. Everyone agreed that indeed we *had* to, and running water was of prime importance. Naturally, though, we didn't get at it immediately because there were so many other projects in this new life which were commanding our first attention. So all year 'round we hauled that beautiful crystal-clear water from the Manson for drinking purposes, and we found it fairly easy to keep buckets of it on hand for daily kitchen usage; but prodigious amounts of water for laundry and bathing were something else. Within a few weeks we had devised a system of catching and containing rainwater from off the roof, but during dry seasons we had to drive two-hundred yards down the hill to fill the galvanized bathtub and boilers from little Slate Creek. By parking on the bridge and dropping a pail on the end of a rope, it was relatively simple to fill a lot of containers. In winter we had to go the more tedious route of melting ice and snow. I came to realize the truth of something Maggie Westfall told me the day we first met her. I had inquired in bewilderment how they were managing without running water, and how they could all keep so clean personally, and maintain so spotless a home. She laughed and replied that between daily sponge baths and weekly tub baths they stayed as clean as they felt they needed to be. As for the spotless home, she modestly shrugged and said that it's amazing how far a bucket of water can be stretched.

After the first year of coping with no water taps in the house, we became so used to the routine that it didn't seem drastic anymore. Another year went by, and another, and occasionally different types of running water and pumping systems were discussed and investigated. More years went by, and suddenly the time to leave was upon us. We left the running-water dilemma in the hands of the new owners.

Routine problems involved with northern living, especially in winter time, sometimes called for spartan determination on our part. Periodically all the roofs would need snow-shoveling. Icicle buildup on the eaves would need to be chopped down. Each morning during the worst of winter, solid ice at least two inches thick would have to be broken out of the water-hole in the creek. Regardless of temperature, regular maintenance was required for the generator and heating systems, fuel had to be pumped. Propane tanks needed occasional changing. For some perplexing reason, thirty-below (F.) seemed to accentuate all the snags in most every piece of machinery or mechanical equipment.

The accomplishing of these tasks and solving of problems would normally be automatically assigned to the man of the household because of the heavy-duty nature of the assignments; but in our case the man-of-the-house often wasn't around. When Larry became jade-involved he also became a commuter. He was away from home more than he was there — in summer out in the prospecting fields, and often in winter out in the big city either lining up financing for more jade prospecting, or lining up buyers for the product. We were all agreed that this had to be the way of things since our present and future financial hopes revolved around this semi-precious green stone. But Larry's frequent absence left all these chores in my hands, and the kids and I would struggle to get them accomplished ourselves rather than ask for help. (I've always deplored the "helpless female" role.) Indeed, I was actually grateful that this new jade "thing" was providing Larry with new stimulation and direction. A steady diet of Manson Creek alone would certainly have become hum-drum for him after a couple of years.

Minor day-to-day problems would often arise, and they would be resolved without a second thought. To the best of my recollection there was only one day when so many minor headaches piled up, one on another, that we were almost at our wits' end.

It began with a feverish early-morning bustle of activity in getting the fellows off on a week's prospecting trip, while at the same time processing a seemingly unusual number of store customers. After the men had finally left and business in the store quieted down, the girls and I collapsed with a leisurely cup of coffee. Before many moments, however, someone stopped by who needed to use the radio-phone. When we attempted unsuccessfully to make contact with the outside world, we discovered to our dismay that the unusually wild wind of the previous night had blown over the aerial and rendered the phone temporarily useless. There was nothing we could do about re-securing the thirty-foot-high line, so the traveler had to go on to Germansen to make his call.

Back to the coffee cups again, we decided unanimously that today should be laundry and bath day. Lyn and Les volunteered to get all the water, so out went the bathtub, boilers, and pails to the back of the truck. That was when they discovered the flat tire and also the un-repaired spare. They were disgusted, but determined, and started a water brigade, hauling from the creek. They made about fifteen trips each, carrying two buckets at a time, grumbling and growling all the way, but still determined, and filling every container they could find. Before evening the mountain of laundry had gone through the washer and was hanging on every available clothesline in town, and each of us had also been processed through the bathtub.

While all this was going on, I had made a trip to the store during the afternoon and noticed the tell-tale presence of propane fumes. That means that the tank for the refrigerator has run out, the gas flame is out, and the residue of propane is coming through unburned. Replacing the empty tank with a full one involves jockying the hundred-pound cylinder into place and hooking it up with a wrench, a bit of muscle, and a little growling.

The final coup to end a perfect (?) day was the moment when we had guests sitting around waiting for the coffee pot to finish perking, and the flame on the Coleman stove fizzled out because the tank had run out of fuel!

Although the day seemed to be one struggle after another, still a great deal was accomplished, in a mood of defiance, if nothing else. But a brilliant way of easing our work-load occurred to me, and I wondered why I hadn't thought of it before. In the future we would box up the soiled linens from the cabins, as well as our own household sheets and towels, and send them out once a week to be done up at the Fort St. James laundry. The freight man could return them to us on his weekly trips, all clean and ready to stack in the linen closet. Happy day! After that momentous decision we seldom ever again washed a sheet, pillow-slip, tea towel, bath towel or hand towel. The few dollars it cost to send them out was paid happily and willingly.

We worked out our problems — they weren't really all that devastating. But the big surprise in all this for me was in the realization that with or without Larry, the family and I were thriving on the unique combination of excitement and contentment which this totally different northern environment was providing. The good aspects outweighed the bad, by far.

*   *   *   *   *   *

As isolated as we thought we were, problems which involved the outside world cropped up now and then. We were once advised by our freight man that word had gotten out that we were bootlegging liquor up here. Heavens! Bootlegging? Us? We had, indeed, ordered a few cases of beer every so often, added only the freight charges to the price, and kept them available for a select few whom we felt like selling them to. Technically we knew that was illegal, and we could have gotten around "the letter of the law" by giving the beer away with the unspoken understanding that the receiving party give us a monetary donation in return. Rather than go through all that hassle, however, and incurring the risk of deportation if the matter were pursued, we merely cut out that item entirely. People would just have to bring their own liquid refreshment, or order it from the freight man themselves.

On another occasion I received a communication from the Vancouver postal headquarters that they had received a counterfeit ten dollar bill in one of my remittances, and that I, as Postmaster, was to be held accountable. I was ordered to write a letter of explanation which would be forwarded to the Committee on Accountability in the Federal Building in Ottawa. It was also suggested that I cooperate fully with the R.C.M.P. who would be in to investigate. It was to be my responsibility to replace the ten dollars to balance our postal money drawer until a decision on the situation should be reached.

Well, we all laughed as we scanned the columns of counterfeit serial numbers which I was supposed to have had at my fingertips. But after the laughter died down, still the officials had to be satisfied. My letter of explanation stated that there were then only about fifteen people in our community, all of whom, living here for many years, were known to be respectable citizens. If any fraudulent money had come into our town, it must have been brought in from the outside, perhaps even unintentionally, and might have passed in and out of our cash drawer and into the hands of one person after another without anyone realizing what he was handling.

Their letter of accusation had arrived in the November mail, and since winter was again upon us, we were not visited by any officials. But it took about nine months for the government wheels to turn to get the matter settled. Their next letter was kinder and more personal. They agreed with me that the money had most probably been accepted innocently, but any repetition of the matter would be dealt with more harshly. I was advised to read and study the lists of counterfeit serial numbers which are sent to every postmaster periodically. I was also sent the ten dollars worth of postal supplies.

Although the mail delivery system never failed us completely, still this was our most frequent headache situation. Days and days were lost while we expected the mail in and it didn't get here. An airline company had the mail contract in the beginning, and although delivery was set for a certain day, weather conditions often caused delays. Then Russell's freight service took over and began bringing the mail along with the regular truck deliveries in summer, and by Sno-Cat in winter. The trucks were quite dependable, but during winter months we'd never know whether the Sno-Cat was going to arrive in the morning or at night, or on precisely which day. In the restlessness of anticipation, hours and days were wasted, and nothing much accomplished except a lot of coffee drinking and socializing with the other residents who were also waiting.

Much of our shopping was done by mail, and after a few years I considered myself quite proficient in this type of ordering. We had catalogues for clothing, household furnishings, tools, car parts, etc. Anything which the catalogues didn't cover could be obtained by simply writing a letter to the appropriate outlet and requesting the needed item to be sent in to us by mail and C.O.D. We had made a few trips to the Fort, to Vanderhoof, and to Prince George, so were acquainted with the types of stores available, and could address a letter to a drug store, a stationery store, a veterinarian, or whomsoever. Over the years I became quite a consumer advisor to anyone who asked where he should send for some particular item. I had no control over what would be sent to fill the order, however. About forty percent of the time we would receive precisely what we had asked for.

*   *   *   *   *   *

The car problems we experienced were not our own, but we were often called on to assist in the solving of other people's. It's hard to believe how many travelers start up this long road completely unprepared for emergencies. It's over a hundred miles of isolated driving from the Fort, with not a commercial rest stop along the way, and indeed, not even a cabin or house anywhere except a very tiny settlement in the area of Nation River. It makes very good sense to have any vehicle equipped with a basic tool kit for any kind of driving anywhere; but when one anticipates a trip up this road, not only the basics should be considered, but also a first aid kit, a food box, sleeping bag or blankets, even an axe and shovel. I suppose it would be hard to believe that some motorists have discovered too late that they didn't even have a car-jack with them. It has happened, and more time than just once.

The only consolation for a motorist in distress is that people do drive the road in summertime, and there may not be too long a wait before someone comes by. Fortunately, almost everyone who drives this road is compassionate enough to stop and render assistance, loan a tool, or if all else fails, drive the stranded motorist to one end of the line or the other. I'll never forget the motorist whose car had suffered a breakdown about thirty miles back, and while he was waiting for someone to come along he decided to build a fire. He gathered together leaves and twigs, but couldn't find anything in the way of paper to wad up except a five dollar bill. He used it, and laughed about it later as he was telling us the adventure.

*   *   *   *   *   *

Sometimes people will ask if the wild animals of the area give us any trouble. Well . . . while we occasionally spot the tracks of moose, lynx, bear, or wolverine on the paths outside of town, and sometimes we see evidence that a moose has crossed the road right inside the "city limits", still the wild animals don't seem interested in invading the inhabited areas or in creating problems with human beings . . . usually.

Untamed animals are very much creatures of instinct, and the changing seasons influence their living habits in the same regular patterns year after year. Therefore, an unseasonably heavy snowfall which dumped two feet of fluffy snow one early week in October must have completely confused one particular grizzly bear about where his hibernation den was, and why he wasn't in it. Or perhaps instinct told him he'd waited too long to fatten up for the long winter sleep, so he'd better look for food in the quickest possible manner. Our first awareness of an intruder in town was King's frantic non-stop barking during one entire night. Next morning there were bear and dog tracks everywhere, circling every cabin and structure in town, and a moose-quarter was gone from a tree where some hunters had hung their recent kill.

There was much gathering together of residents to talk this over, compare notes, and decide what — if anything — should be done. We decided to lay low, but to be prepared if our visitor should return with evil intent.

The second night was a repetition of the first. As soon as King started up the growly barking we knew the bear was back and was making the rounds. Everyone had gone to bed with rifles at the ready, but no one slept much that night. Nor was anyone eager to fire a shot in the dark, perhaps only to wound the animal and then be faced with an angry, hurt bear who might either attack with intent, or else take off into the bush and be difficult and dangerous to track to the finish. No one stayed alone that night either. No one except Ernie, that is. Ernie, our prospector friend, who lives about a half-mile from town came rushing up next morning to tell us that the bear had been thrashing around in his woodshed the night before. He had shone a powerful flashlight beam at the animal, and had fired two warning shots. Nothing seemed to faze that bear. It ambled away when it was ready to go, and not before.

We had all heard the bear around our own cabins, snorting and pawing, knocking over pails, boxes, and just generally making himself completely at home all around town. After two nights of this, it was our unanimous decision to call in the game warden and let him handle the situation in professional style. We made the phone call, and the warden arrived the same day and went into immediate action. He told us to keep all dogs and cats inside during the night because he was going to put out a chunk of meat injected with a powerful bear poison. The job was accomplished promptly. The dead animal was found not too far from town next morning, but his furry coat had already been removed by opportunists who knew that a silver-tip grizzly pelt was worth four-hundred dollars at the time! The warden was horrified. He said that if the skinners had gotten even a trace of that poisoned blood or flesh into any tiny cut or wound on themselves, they'd be mighty sick individuals.

It didn't take much sleuthing to locate the pelt, and after issuing a stern reprimand, the warden relieved them of their dangerous prize and burned it along with the carcass and as much of the raked-together mess as could be retrieved. Blood and bits of flesh were too widespread, however, and one of the local dogs found a little which had been overlooked. He died a quick and severe death. The Game Warden, our friend, had intended a swift and clean elimination of our problem. He shook his head in sad dismay and said once again that it isn't the animals but the irresponsible humans who give him the most trouble.

On this last point we readily concurred. Several years ago we had done an about-face in our attitude about hunters and hunting. The invasion of gun-wielders every September and October is anticipated with dread not just by us, but by most every resident of the North. One particular opening day of hunting season was ushered in at Manson with the sound of a horrible, shuddering crash. We all ran outside, and there was our store porch shoved three feet to the left by a car whose driver neglected to apply brakes soon enough as he was pulling up beside the gas pump.

The only slightly chagrined fellow called out as we approached, "Hello there, Owens! Remember me?" Then he gestured at the misplaced log porch and grinned. "I'm sorry about thish. My buddy and I'll get it back in place."

So far we hadn't seen anyone else around, but our "friend" maneuvered his way back to the car with some difficulty, and called to his buddy who had passed out in the back seat.

"Hey, Joe, wake up man. We got a job to do here."

"Wha . . . Whassat? Where're we?" came the slurred voice inside.

"Hey, come on, Joe. We gotta fix sumthin'. I ran into the porch here. Geddup, Joe, you gotta help me."

Larry had been patient with the fellows and we just stood by to see what they were going to accomplish. They both looked the problem over, staggered a bit from one end of the porch to the other, taking stock of the situation. Their decision was to tie a rope around the bottom log and pull the entire structure back in place with their car providing the muscle. To our surprise it worked, and didn't take long to accomplish, either. The two drunks decided they'd be nice and rent a cabin from us. We decided they wouldn't, however, and told them there were none available. Actually there were, but that ever-present fear of careless action around gas lamps and wood stoves has taught us to be discriminating about cabin-rentals.

Before traveling on, the friendly twosome offered us a guzzle from their almost-empty bottle. We declined, but as they drove off we shrugged and reminded ourselves that here we go again . . .

Not more than a week later we were startled at the sound of something roaring and clanking its way into town from the Germansen Lake direction. As it passed by and pulled up at the gas pump, we thought it was a pickup truck, but the dreadful clouds of smoke from the exhaust almost obscured it completely. I thought it was going to explode for sure!

The three jaunty hunters were completely sober, and didn't seem terribly worried about their truck's distress. They said that someone must have put diesel into their spare gas cans back there in Vanderhoof where they filled up last. It didn't take me long to decide that if they'd really been served diesel when they wanted gas, they'd be hopping mad and ready to sue the gas station. I couldn't accuse them, of course, but I knew they must have helped themselves to what they thought was gas, somewhere up the road.

Sure enough, a few days later one of our hunting guides stopped by and told us of watching a bunch of fellows, through binoculars, as they siphoned some of his diesel into their truck and their spare gas cans. He hadn't driven over and interrupted the theft because the thought of what was going to happen to their truck motor amused him. I told the guide they'd made it this far in a horrible cloud of smoke, and that they'd filled up with gas here, hoping to dilute what diesel was left in the tank. I suppose they made it back out of the country because we heard no more about this particular truck. I must admit that I, too, was sadly amused.

144

I usually try to avoid generalizing and pidgeon-holing people, but from firsthand experience and observation, I regret to say that road-hunters, with only a few exceptions, fall into one unfortunate category. We all dread hunting season and everyone plans to stay at home or have someone else on the premises if they have to be away at this time. Unoccupied cabins have been ransacked, pot-shots go zinging through windows of apparently deserted buildings. One happy-go-lucky bunch of drinking buddies had set up a target right at a bend in the road, and were shooting at it. They probably thought they were at the end of nowhere, but they most certainly weren't. Friends of ours had rounded that bend between shots, fortunately, and were horrified to contemplate what might have happened. It was incredible to think that any group of grown men could be so entirely irresponsible. Hopefully, it won't be long before there is a change in the regulations which allow just anyone who is capable of writing his name on the dotted line to be granted a license to carry and use a lethal weapon. Probably only the noisy five percent of all hunters fall into this totally reckless category, but we know they're there because we see them every year.

Another five percent at the other end of the scale are the genuine sporting hunters who are killing the animal for the meat. We see these every year, too, and some are family friends whom we look forward to seeing on their annual excursions.

The other vast ninety percent, however, are guilty of one or more of the following sins: the trophy hunter who cuts down the biggest and best of the species, taking only the rack of horns and leaving the meat to rot; the poor-vision enthusiast who fires at anything he sees moving in the bush; the idiot who shoots an animal across a lake with no thought for how he's going to retrieve it; the "hunter" who wounds an animal and doesn't track it to the finish; the sport who considers a hunting trip an excuse to get away from home and family for a week-long drinking spree. There's one more — the well-intentioned hunter who kills for the meat, gets it home into the freezer, but somehow doesn't get much of it eaten so that in the next spring's housecleaning efforts a good portion of the game meat is thrown out. The transgressions are many. We see and hear about them year after year. To our great surprise there were no gun-involved hunting accidents, but some of us participated in a few searches for hunters who got themselves lost up in our area of the woods.

*　　*　　*　　*　　*　　*

What perplexes most inquiring tourists is the matter of how the man of the family is supposed to earn a living way out in this wilderness, and many have wistfully stated that they'd love to live here as we do, but couldn't consider it without an assured monthly income. A few individuals have even driven up the long road for the express purpose of looking around for some kind of work, and state that they will happily move here if they could find work. This is a logical, normal and noble approach to job-hunting in the city, but it will lead to nothing in the north woods. One must want so intensely to get away from things urban that nothing else matters, and then somehow it all works out. Aside from one couple who arrived on the scene with a small inherited fortune at their disposal, few if any of the families or individuals who gravitated up our way of live, during our ten years of observation, came with a job lined up. And in truth there aren't any "jobs", as such, to be applied for. After one has made the decision to migrate to the North, moves in and gets settled and begins to be known in the area, then it all happens. In summertime some of the men and older boys are hired to work with the road and bridge crews. Mining companies usually bring in their own men, but vacancies invariably develop, and frequently local men will be hired. The forestry recruits men for fire-fighting, and game guides sometimes are on the lookout for willing and eager trainees. Fellows who live here in the bush usually make better and more contented workers than the "imported" city boys who too soon miss the bright lights and action.

Actually it costs far less to live up here, too. I shall never forget a comment made by a father who, with his wife and children, had been camping at one of the local lakes. On their way home they stopped in at the store for gas and for a few goodies to nibble on during the long drive.

As he reached for his wallet he said in great wonderment, "We've been at the lake for a week now, and today is the first time I've had my hand in my pocket for money. You know, I don't believe there's been another week like that in my entire adult life."

A tourist looking at the price of our gas and groceries would be tempted to hoot and howl at my statement about our cost-of-living, but I stand by it nonetheless. While things we handle do, of course, cost far more than in a supermarket, still one spends less on his over-all grocery bill because in no way is he tempted to over-buy. The supermarket abundance and variety of items is just not there to be tempting. Cooking and eating are more basic here. And with no rent to pay, no light, heat, gas, water, or phone bills, and no eternal charge account payments which invariably accompany urban living, I defy anyone to prove that he can't live here as he'd like to because he can't afford it. This being the case, there isn't the need of the accustomed big monthly pay cheque.

*   *   *   *   *   *

146

Having left the big city and all its accompanying locks and keys behind, it was refreshing to have found a part of the world where we could go to bed at night and leave the doors unlocked without losing a wink of sleep over it. Recalling when we first came here and wondered about Mr. Hamilton and his cumbersome key chain, we never did figure why he was so fearful. For a while we locked the store and our own front door at night, but after getting to know the people and the pulse of the area, it seemed foolish. For a few years we were actually leaving the store door standing open all night for ventilation in summer, with only the screen door hooked on the outside to keep out dogs, cats, and squirrels. Everyone has heard about the remote northern trail cabins where a traveller could stop in to rest and warm himself, make a cup of tea and even expect to find some basic nourishment. There was an unspoken understanding that what a man needed he was welcome to; but he would leave a note of thanks, a pile of cut wood to replace what he'd used, sometimes even money, and then go on his way refreshed.

Beautiful situations like that were doomed, however. There was a change taking place everywhere and it happened during the years of the sixties. We could sense it gradually creeping in, and we knew when the time had come to start locking the doors. Perhaps it was attributable to the fact that by this time the North wasn't that remote anymore. C'est la vie.

Stan Enters the Scene 29

Prospectors seldom go out into the hills alone anymore. The dangers of tangling with a grizzly, breaking a leg by tripping over a half-buried tree root, losing one's sense of direction, or of falling prey to any number of potential dangers makes the wisdom of two-man teams the rule rather than the exception. Nature in the wilds is nothing to take lightly. So after Robert and Carolyn left us to return to the States, Larry was in need of a new prospecting partner.

As was customary each spring, we'd all tackle the annual "clean up, paint up, fix up, build up" with the usual enthusiasm, but Larry's eagerness to get the jobs done was probably a salving of conscience since I knew that his plans for summer did not include spending time waiting on customers and talking to tourists. He was itching to get out into the hills and he'd find a way — partner or no partner. Knowing and living with Larry's restless spirit for so many years past, I could tell that his main interest in Manson was rapidly becoming that of a convenient launching pad for his summer prospecting trips. He was almost totally involved with rocks and minerals, and truly seemed bored with almost everything else. Coffee sessions, which were still frequent with old friends and new, would always start out in a general way, conversationally, but invariably would drift into mining subjects. This change of pace was really getting to Lyn. She'd recognize the turning point and give me that hopeless look which said, "Here we go again," as she'd leave the room in search of a more stimulating activity. I'll have to admit that even I had the feeling that Larry, who had always been so witty and brilliant, was rapidly developing a one-track mind. But I also knew that I couldn't, and wouldn't even try, to thwart this new trend of his learning.

About this time Ernie Floyd, one of our summer residents and a long-time prospector at Manson, came back in for the year's field activities, bringing with him a mining man he had met and become acquainted with during the winter. Our first reaction to this new man was one of friendliness and warmth, since somehow we could immediately sense hidden depths behind the dark eyes, cultured voice, and educated words. It was impossible to figure his age because a full black beard partially covered his face. I guessed him to be around forty-five. He seemed to know a great deal about a lot of things, and had traveled rather extensively through Canada, the States, and Mexico.

Since Ernie was an almost daily visitor to our house, so also was this new friend, Stan Porayko. Larry had now attained the ultimate in happiness because the three fellows talked "rocks and minerals" and drank coffee by the hour, day after day.

Ernie and Stan made many prospecting trips that summer, and often they included Larry since he was an eager man in the field. But before long, Ernie could sense that he was losing Stan to Larry, for the two younger men were poring over maps and making elaborate plans for the following summer. Ernie was not unhappy over this new development because he himself was approaching retirement age, and his greatest joy was to have a part in starting or encouraging younger men along the same rocks-and-minerals road he had traveled for so many years.

Stan's mining interests had always been in jade and other gemstones, and since jade had already been found on Kwanika, the two men started from that spot on mineral maps, outlining areas for investigation during the next few years. But right now they were so eager that although it was already mid-October and the first few snows had fallen and melted, the fellows hurriedly put together camp supplies for a week-long trip into the area they had marked on the map, in order to do a quick surveillance.

They left; but on the day they returned home, there was an incredible story to tell:

After driving as far as the road permitted, they had parked the truck and gone up-river in a fifteen-foot aluminum boat with outboard motor. Their object was to do a quick prospecting of a number of creeks emptying into the Omineca River. All went well and they had gathered lots of samples and made notes for specific spots to investigate more thoroughly next year. The homeward trip down-stream, however, was another story. Somewhere along the way the boat struck an underwater snag and upended so suddenly that they were floundering around in the almost-freezing water before they knew what had happended. Stan swam for the nearby shore, and Larry went after the boat which was bobbing along and moving steadily away from him. About a quarter-mile later, Stan helped both Larry and the boat out onto the riverbank, and with a trusty supply of waterproof matches, got a bonfire going in short order. Both fellows peeled off right down to bare skin. The air wasn't all that warm, but the wet clothes were worse. Larry was so cold and his teeth chattered so vigorously and uncontrollably that when Stan lit a cigarette for him and stuck it in his mouth, he involuntarily bit it in half!

After a few hours, when clothes were dry and the chills a bit lessened, the hardy prospectors put the boat into the water again. The outboard motor had been damaged, so with the help of one oar, they had to drift the several miles back to where the truck had been left. Lost forever somewhere in the Omineca River were a camera, a rifle, all their camp supplies, sleeping bags, and food. But worst of all — all the beautiful rock samples they'd gathered were at the bottom of the river — somewhere.

The men arrived home voraciously hungry and certain that they'd not be warmed through thoroughly for another week at least.

The telling, re-living, and laughing over this experience brought Stan closer into the family circle. In the beginning he'd been Larry's friend, but now we were all enjoying his sense of humor and his light-hearted disposition. Lyn and Les were even discovering that he wasn't as totally a rocks-and-minerals man as they had thought. In fact, their association became so friendly that they actually talked Stan into letting them shave off his beard. This was considered to be a monumental victory by the girls because they knew that a man who has nurtured and lived with his beard for three years isn't going to part with it lightly.

A date for this great event was set, and when the evening arrived, Lyn and Les had made extensive preparations. A chair had been set up under the light, and in readiness were combs, scissors, a razor and lots of blades, shave cream, towels, hot water, and even an assortment of reading material for the "victim" to amuse himself with while the operators were working. For some reason all mirrors in the room had either been covered or put out of sight.

Stan appeared at the door, right on time and still willing. No time was wasted. The girls set him down, draped a huge towel around his neck, and went to work immediately. Off came handfuls of the coarse black hair which the "barbers" were attacking with scissors first. Then they lathered him up and started shaving off the remaining stubble. A full package of blades later, we were astounded to see the youthfulness which was revealed to us. More than ten years came off with that beard, and Stan admitted that he was really only thirty-two years old!

By now winter was just around the corner and most of the summer people had already left for the year. Stan was making his own plans, and under Larry's eager encouragement, was thinking seriously of taking up permanent year-round residence at Manson Creek. He enjoyed our

150

way of life, loved the natural beauty of the area, and since he was unattached and independent, the change could easily be accomplished. The two men were good prospecting partners and felt they were on the track of something good. It didn't take long to cinch the decision. Stan would go back down south for the coming winter and work and save money while disposing of his trailer-home and other unnecessary possessions. Early the next summer he'd return, prepared to move into one of our cabins and start a new life from the vantage point of Manson Creek.

Every Prospector's Dream 30

Larry and Stan corresponded during that winter, sharing thoughts and ideas about jade prospecting. The following summer Stan moved up to Manson, exactly as he said he would, with no more possessions than he could carry with him in his Jeep. He settled into one of our rental cabins and we were all delighted to have him now a real part of our little community.

The fellows didn't waste much time, though. Maps were brought out and they began planning possible areas for investigation. They were thinking about going farther back into the bush than where they had hurriedly looked the previous year. The goal-area they finally set their sights on was Ogden Mountain which, on the mineral map, showed two parallel ribbons of serpentine (the parent mineral of jade) through its massive bulk. This new destination would be no easy venture. There would be a sixty-mile trip by truck, and then a twenty-mile hike through bush and swamp with all their supplies and gear in packs on their backs. Although getting there would present some difficulties, still Ogden Mountain looked promising on the mineral map. Another factor influencing the decision was that being so remote, it most likely would be an untramped area, which most of this gold mining country certainly wasn't!

After much preparation and elimination of everything but absolute essentials, including two weeks' supply of dehydrated food, they took off. The first leg of the trip was an uneventful few hours by truck; but after they had parked the vehicle and continued on foot, it was another story. The warm, moist air was alive with tiny vicious black flies and mosquitoes. Swamp areas presented real difficulties. The men were chopping paths through devil's club as tall as their heads, but were constantly veering toward Ogden Mountain which loomed just ahead of them. It took four days of their precious two weeks' time just to break trail along the plotted course.

On the fifth day they reached the foot of the mountain and came upon Ogden Creek whose noisy waters tumbled down the rugged slopes of the hill. Here they decided to make the base camp from which all prospecting would be done. An area was cleared, firewood for a few days cut and stacked, the lightweight silk tent erected and supper cooked and eaten. The men fought the urge to begin studying the rocks in the creek that evening. Their first thought was that they might be disappointed, and they didn't need that kind of letdown so soon. But all night the creek babbled endlessly, teasing them about its undiscovered secrets.

Next morning, after breakfast and a quick camp cleanup, they started walking upstream along the creek, checking rocks as they went. Within a half-hour they came across the first prize. It was a beautiful, brilliant, water-polished, 250 pound green rock which lay in the shallow water. Not even an amateur rockhound could have passed it by. For identification and referral purposes, and in honor of its magnificent green, they named it "Kelly One." A few hours later and another mile upstream, to their amazement, they came across "Kelly Two." From here on, the jade rocks were as commonplace as granite, although not of the outer beauty and apparent quality of the first two Kellys. In one stretch of two hundred yards they could jump from one jade boulder to another without stepping on any other type of rock. The creek was a bonanza! Unfortunately, however, the sizes of the boulders were staggering. Many were estimated at five-hundred to a thousand-pound bulks, and some were even calculated in tonnage. There was enough jade in the creek to satisfy a lifetime of cutting and selling!

After staking claims to completely cover the choice spots of the creek and surrounding areas, and after spending another two days clearing a helicopter site and hauling Kellys I and II by litter back to the site, Larry and Stan returned to Manson Creek jubilant. All they needed now was about a hundred thousand dollars to set up a mining, cutting and transporting operation! Somehow, to them the prospect of overcoming this small stumbling block didn't seem too impossible since the presence of the product was already assured; but a lot of leg-work and contacts out in the big city were going to be required.

But meanwhile Kellys I and II were sitting at the helicopter site sixty air miles away, awaiting transportation back to Manson. We were all completely unaccustomed to air travel and air transport expenses, so the prospect of putting out six-hundred dollars for two hours of helicopter work in bringing two hunks of rock back to Manson was staggering. At that particular time, six hundred might as well have been six thousand to our thin bank account which went up and down with store sales.

The first "investor" who came to our rescue and put up the needed cash (with no strings attached except repayment in jade) was a brand new friend who had just moved into our town. He was intrigued with Larry and Stan's prospects and happily and willingly offered the six hundred dollars for the helicopter time.

I must admit that any doubts I might have had were cast aside when I viewed those two beautiful green rocks which were deposited in our yard. I'd never seen jade that was completely green on the outside, having had all its outer crust worn off by centuries of water action in the creek. Still, with jade, the proof of quality lies inside the rock, and is revealed only by cutting it in half. No time was wasted in setting up the saw, and when the cutting proved exactly what we all were hoping, the only thing left to do then was to make up a ringstone. To the jubilant satisfaction of everyone, Kelly I was nothing but 270 pounds of superb, translucent, light green British Columbia jade, and the first few sales netted forty dollars per pound! Kelly II was even more intensely green, but it was badly fractured inside. We concentrated our attention on Number One.

After a few weeks Stan and Larry went back to Ogden, flying their camp in by bush-plane this time, and landing on Ogden Lake. It took them ten days to cut a trail from the lake up to the top of the mountain, but this time it was with real purpose and intent. Now they could approach their creek from its source at the top and work downward. In short order the 24-inch saw was set up to start cutting down through a huge boulder which lay there in the creek looking quite worthwhile. That year the fellows did everything the hard way, keeping expenses down to a minimum. Each morning they would haul fuel down to the saw; each evening they'd haul the blocks of cut jade back to camp. They knew enough about their product to have figured that it was economically smart to cut and sort the jade on the spot since they'd be paying air-freight charges on whatever was brought out. In this they were so right. One sixteen-ton boulder which looked promising on the outside proved worthless when cut in half.

By the time the snows were falling it took them two days of continuous transporting to move everything from the top of the mountain back down their trail to the lake which was twenty-five hundred feet below. From there the bush-plane brought them and the fruits of their labors back to Manson.

Early summer of the next year 1968, the entire work party, which consisted of a couple more men, 36-inch saws, fuel, food, tents, etc., was flown in by helicopter right to the top camp on Ogden. It was a good work season, and when October rolled around there was about thirteen tons of excellent jade in hundred-pound blocks ready to come out.

For identification of the cut pieces, a naming and numbering system was devised. The more outstanding rocks (such as Kelly I and II) were always considered worthy of a name, and spontaneously appropriate titles were applied, such as "Super Kelly", "Fantastic Kelly", "Six-Tonner", "Twelve-Tonner", "Peace on Earth", "Jolly Green Giant", and others.

By this time, faith in Larry and Stan's newly found jade field was being evidenced by one of our interior bush-plane companies. Northern Mountain Airline worked out a plan which could most efficiently and least expensively move the product from Ogden to Manson. They also offered to let us delay payment until sufficient jade sales made it easier. The way they worked it out, the operation would utilize a plane-helicopter combination effort. When the cutting season was over, the "chopper" would work continuously at ferrying the heavy blocks of jade from Ogden's top, down to the newly-built dock on the lake below — a five-minute hop. Working completely independently, a Beaver (fixed-wing aircraft) would carry 1700-pound payloads of jade blocks from Ogden Lake to Wolverine Lake — a 25-minute trip. Our man at Wolverine would then truck the blocks back to Manson, a three-mile ride. Using a long, horizontal ladder-type device with rollers as "steps", the jade could be moved on and off the plane and trucks with a minimum of handling. That year twenty-six thousand pounds of beautiful green rock was transported in five days of concentrated effort, and in the most economical way which could have been devised. But still this wasn't the end of the line. All this tonnage had to be transferred six-hundred miles via two freight lines from Manson to Vancouver if it was to be sold and shipped around the world. In truth, freight costs were a staggering item in the total operation, but there was just no other way.

During that winter contacts were made and Ogden Mountain Jade was being heard about and was appearing on the world scene: Red China, Germany, the United States, and in Canada.

But the story didn't end there.

It was during the 1969 work season that the really great discovery was made. This year more men, more saws, more camp supplies and a core-drill for pre-testing the interior of rocks, were all flown in to Ogden early in the season for the short three-month period of intense work before snowfall and freezeup, both of which happen early in October at this higher elevation. After everything was set up and work well underway, Stan and Larry would often take a prospecting trip off in one direction or another from camp. They had speculated on the likelihood of finding jade-in-place — where it was actually formed many millions of years ago — the "mother lode." They had discussed the possibility, but had not wasted time groping around on mountainsides looking for it because they felt that it would be buried inside the mountain under too much overburden. It seemed far more logical to satisfy themselves with the exposed jade in creek beds.

But on one of their prospecting trips around the mountain one day, they came face to face with a rock outcropping at the edge of a meadow. Dozens of large and small boulders were scattered about, some of them buried with just their tops showing, while others of considerable bulk stood four or five feet tall. Most dramatic of all was a fourteen-foot vertical face of rock which, after soil and debris was cleared from around it, proved to be twenty-four feet long and of undetermined depth into the mountain. From a distance they had thought it was granite, but both realized at the same moment that it wasn't. They put the drill to work immediately and the four-inch extracted cores were a beautiful bright green. Moving around in the area they took random samples from every visible rock. Most of them were beautiful, and some better than others. They realized that here before them was a massive show of jade never before seen anywhere in the world.

The men were speechless while their minds were working overtime. Stan had always said that the most he'd ever wish for was to find a small mineral property rich in resources which he could work two or three times a year for a living. Larry knew that the odds of a prospector ever striking it rich were a million to one, but here they'd gone and done it!

To obtain an independent professional opinion a geologist from Vancouver was invited to go to Ogden Mountain to assess the discovery. He was helicoptered to Ogden from Manson, and upon his return he entered our house with his head bowed and stated very sincerely and solemnly that it had been a rare privilege for him to have witnessed such a fantastic showing.

Kuan-Yin Smiles 31

There are those who, in disgruntled tones, have voiced their fear that this jade discovery will flood the market, thereby cheapening the value of the product. Certainly there will be more jade available to more people, but the market will not be flooded. The remoteness of the mine site, the difficulties involved in flying the total working camp in and out for only three months of summer operation will, in itself, ensure against an over-abundance of the product on the market at any time.

As to cost, jade will remain a luxury item, but with more people being able to afford the luxury. A square inch (⅜" thick) of the choicest material might sell for three dollars to an individual, while a wholesale buyer might be paying three dollars a pound buying in hundred-pound blocks. There are so many grades of the material available for different usages, and the price for a ton, a pound, or a slice will naturally vary with the quantity desired. It is difficult to sketch out a simplified price structure where jade is concerned. But at least it will always be available now to any who have a desire to own a bit of it.

There are also those who, by fair means or foul, must worm their way into an act when an opportunity presents itself. We unwittingly provided the opportunity by failing to fence-in the area of our outdoor jade-cutting operation at Manson. The circular diamond saws grinding their way through huge green blocks were a familiar sight in the yard adjacent to our home, and the public seemed to appreciate watching and talking about everything concerning this fascinating operation.

We were too trusting. One morning Evy came running in the back door and said that our wheelbarrow was way down the back path, tipped over, and a big jade block lying beside it. That seemed strange since the cutting crew had been working out there the day before, and the wheelbarrow was a much-used piece of equipment. I went out to see for myself if what I feared had actually happened. Sure enough, about a hundred yards down the back hill was the evidence, just as Ev had stated, but also in the immediate area of the cutting works there were a lot of vacant spots where chunks of jade had sat. I sent Evy on the run to fetch Stan from his cabin across the creek, and it was Stan's guess that at least a ton of choice cut-down blocks had been thieved, plus a couple of saw frames and the circular diamond-studded blades.

It was easy to retrace the crime. Truck tracks were visible leaving the road and coming through the brush to the bottom of the hill behind our property. We kicked ourselves for being so negligent, but it never even occurred to us to take such precautions. About then we realized how unconsciously we had depended on King to do all the watch-dogging duties around the place, and he had always obliged. But King was honorably excused this time. A few days before he had partially crippled himself in an awkward leap off the back of the truck. We had been letting him sleep inside by the stove because it was late in the year and nighttime temperatures were already approaching the freezing point.

Stan made a radio-phone call to Larry who was in Vancouver at the time, and then he phoned the R.C.M.P. to report the theft. The police flew in immediately to assess the situation, ask questions, and take notes. There wasn't much else they could do at the scene of the crime.

We weren't short of jade. There was still a lot of it sitting around the yard, and plenty more up on Ogden Mountain. But Stan's legitimate anger was over the fact that after he and Larry had done all the prospecting and made the discovery, suffered all the headaches and leg aches in getting things to the point they were, a bunch of thieves now had a substantial quantity of the product all ready for market, and handed to them on the proverbial silver platter.

What the crooks didn't realize, however, is that the world of wholesale jade buyers and dealers is relatively small. A good jade-man can recognize and identify almost any piece of the superb quality material as a product from a certain area in the world, in the same way that raw gold can be pin-pointed, location-wise, by anyone who has spent his working years with gold, and has observed the identifying shades, colors, and other minute distinguishing factors.

So after the thieves got the loot down to Vancouver and into the backyard and cellar of a partner in crime, they started making their contacts for sale. One of the buyers they invited knew Larry and Stan, and knew that a quantity of their jade had been stolen. He went over to see Larry, and together they set up an arrangement where Larry would pose as an interested buyer.

It was incredibly, unbelievably simple. The two men arrived, were shown the display, recognized it, left on some pretence or other to get the police into the act, and the case went to court.

But in another completely different situation, the offending party didn't get off so easily. In fact, he lost his life. This jade buyer wanted a quantity of the green rock, so he flew his private plane from his home in the States up to Prince George, and hired a bush plane to bring him right up to Manson. He spent the best part of the day choosing and marking the blocks he wanted, then flew back to Prince George to await delivery of his purchase which would be air-freighted out by a heavy-duty Beaver craft.

When his order arrived, he checked it over, claimed that it was two blocks short, and demanded another air trip to bring out his complete order. We knew he had received what he'd paid for. It had always been our policy to give full measure, plus, when selling jade. But after two or three radio-phone arguments we gave in and arranged the fast air delivery of what our "friend" was demanding.

The blocks of jade which were retrieved from his plane crash indicated that he had had a couple hundred pounds more than he had paid for, and about five hundred pounds more than his small plane was legally supposed to carry.

Details of the tragedy were related to us a short while later. The fellow had transferred the load into his plane, not spacing and balancing the heavy blocks properly. On his take-off down the runway he was warned by the tower that something wasn't right and he should return. He chose to ignore them, however, and continued. Fifty feet in the air the plane nose-dived and crashed at the end of the runway. The man and his companion perished in a fiery holocaust.

Even though we had been a little unhappy with that particular jade sale, we never would have wished such ill luck on anyone. Actually the death of these two men touched us deeply, and struck mighty close to home. They had been our guests and sat at our table only the day before. But try as we might, we couldn't help that mysterious feeling that Kuan-Yin, the protecting goddess of jade so revered by the Chinese people since ancient times, must also be smiling upon Stan and Larry as friendly allies, and heaven help anyone who tries to tamper with their destiny in ungentlemanly ways!

Probably the Best Years   32

During the time of the big jade excitement on Ogden Mountain, life on
the home front was certainly not standing still. Mose definitely not! It
was a period of tremendous growth and activity in the Manson-
Germansen area. More and more tourists, prospectors, hunters,
fishermen, and family campers were coming north, since each year the
road was being pushed farther and farther toward its eventual joining
with the Alaskan Highway. The north country was opening up, and
these were exciting times to be part of the activity.

If you were to ask any member of the Owen family which were the
best years of our decade at Manson, each one would undoubtedly say,
"Oh, probably around 1968, '69 and '70," and each opinion would reflect
different reasons. For Larry, of course, the jade-find overshadowed
anything else which had ever happened in any way to touch his life.
Newspaper articles on the subject were appearing in many papers
across Canada and the States. Since the successful prospectors were
mentioned by name, a few of our friends spotted the items and sent
them to us with comments such as "Congratulations, and goodbye to the
peaceful life", or "Imagine my surprise to find this item in our local
paper (in Texas)!" Closer to home one Prince George newspaper
headlined "$40 MILLION JADE FIND IN B.C." in bold black letters.
It took us a while to figure how the reporter could have come up with
that particular amount. Two thousand tons of the rock at ten dollars a
pound would do it, not considering the vast mining, transporting, and
marketing expenses. But these things must be considered, and also the
fact that at this point no one knows the depth of the jade into the
mountain — not the geologist, not the prospectors, and certainly not the
reporter. Nonetheless, we had a lot of good fun over the forty-million
dollar headline, and it was the motivation behind much tourist
comment.

For Lyn and Les, daily living reached an all-time high during these special years. I'm sure that no two girls have ever had so many and varied experiences with so many and varied people — strangers, friends, and admirers.

Of course young Evy wouldn't have an opinion, but I could say that at ages seven and eight he evidenced more maturity and responsibility than many twelve-year-olds.

For myself, I particularly enjoyed the increased activity going on around town and up and down the road. I, too, was involved in the jade operation since Manson Creek was home base — the starting point for each summer's operation and the vital holding area in the transportation scheme for getting the large cut blocks of jade between the mountain site and their semi-final destination in Vancouver. There would always be about a month more working time at our 3000-foot Manson Creek level after winter had struck 5000-foot Mt. Ogden, so the cutting and loading crew required feeding and housing.

During these "special years" several big mining companies were concentrating their exploration teams up in our part of British Columbia. Germansen Landing was selected as their home base since it gave them a twenty-mile head start toward their eventual destinations. That little settlement was bursting at the seams with tents, trailers, and all sorts of temporary housing. Every available cabin had been reserved well in advance of the season, and four or five different airline companies had their helicopters and float planes based there. At eight in the morning and five in the afternoon both sides of the river took on the aspect of busy airfields, as mining crews took off to their various work sites and later returned to camp.

This was the time when the general unrest and moving about of the younger generation brought a number of their "hippy" representatives up our way in their battered trucks, vans, or psychedelic-painted buses. There was unrest among others, too. Within a short space of time six families, totalling about thirty new people, had migrated our way from various points in the States and Canada. The families, one by one, settled along a twenty-mile stretch of river valley northwest of Germansen Landing, and built fine, comfortable homes at approximately three-mile intervals along the north road. But the wandering young people camped temporarily anywhere from the Manson Lakes (fifteen miles south of us), all the way up through Manson and toward Germansen. All these new people were dependent on our road for access and supplies, so we stretched the invisible boundaries of "our area" to cover everyone located along this fifty-mile stretch of road.

It was a period of great influence and observation for Lyn and Les. Being quite aware of the youth rebellion going on in the outside world, they were intrigued by the sights and sounds of the carloads and truckloads of long-haired, scraggly-bearded kids who descended upon our town — all in the typical hippy uniform which consisted of merely appearing to the world in as unkempt and sloppy a manner as was humanly possible. The groups and gangs would always stop at the store to inquire about the location of any old cabins where they could camp. Well . . . the usable cabins belonged to people, and I wouldn't have dreamed of suggesting any of the derelict buildings, so I wasn't of much help them. Undaunted, they'd roam around the back roads until they'd come across some old shack which would barely keep them out of the rain. Their lack of even minimal pride in themselves and their surroundings was appalling. And they evidently had expected to live off the land, because most of them came with practically nothing in the way of money or goods. Groups would come to the store and buy one pound of hamburger and a box of rice or macaroni which, together with a can of tomatoes, would provide a meal for whatever number of kids might gather together that night. Although salad ingredients and fruits were almost always available in the store, these wanderers seldom bought them. A cabbage was cheaper and would go a lot farther. Actually, for food value, their selections weren't too bad, but the number they were feeding on such limited rations could vary from ten to twenty at any one time!

One day when Lyn and I were in the store, one of the groups came with the idea of splurging. They had decided to indulge in a chocolate bar apiece. One of the girls left the candy counter and walked over to look at the fruit table. She gave a long look at a crate of fresh cherries and then picked up a tomato, asking how much one would cost. When the scale read "25c" she calmly put it back and took a ten-cent chocolate bar as the others had, but the momentary look of longing on her face almost tore me to pieces. I had learned by now that she had come from a far better way of life, and I couldn't help wondering if she was weighing what she had given up against the way of life she'd chosen, in the few moments it took to price one tomato.

Of the dozens of kids who descended upon the Manson area, only a few stayed any length of time. Almost without exception they had come from the States, in the cause of avoiding being drafted into the controversial Vietnam conflict. And they had come with the idea of making some kind of a home here, but invariably they'd find something unfavorable: the isolation was too real, permanent housing too much of a problem, the summer season too short, and ground too unfertile. They'd stay a few weeks and then pile into their overflowing vehicles and head out to try somewhere else. The few who stayed behind were always ready to provide open house for the next load of kids who'd arrive. They seemed able to seek each other out as easily as running water finds a downhill course. There was a lot of coming and going for a few summer seasons.

Of course, drugs came in along with the kids. We didn't suspect "hard" drugs, but "grass" and others of the "lesser" evils were as common as they were anywhere else at that time. Lyn and Les were just the right age and could have been prime candidates for the youth movement had they so desired. Fortunately they didn't so desire. Life for them was busy and active enough. They loved good food and clean, warm beds. Somehow scrounging didn't appeal to them. They let their hair grow long, but kept it clean and well groomed. They wore clothes which fit them because they liked it better that way. They benefited from observing their contemporaries who were trying to prove to everyone that they were happy in doing "their thing", but from our front row observation post we somehow felt that it was all a big bluff. It just couldn't be that all these poor young human tramps were actually proud of what they were doing to themselves.

We got to know the ones who stayed around for a while, and found that basically they were "just kids" off on a misdirected course. No one would have guessed the excitement in store, however. Unknown to us all, disguised government officials had been in our midst for a week, and the day they chose to make their round-up we received a note from one of the captives which read:

"Help! We've been busted! Maggie, will you keep our dog until we get further word to you? We're being flown out by the R.C.M.P. Thanks for all past kindnesses."

The young people in custody had been picked up, one by one, and were under guard at Germansen. The officers were checking every hangout which they had previously spotted by air. All the kids were cooperative except one of the boys who had a police record behind him in the States. He took off on the run and had to be rounded up by the trained police dog which accompanied the officers. Of the twenty or thirty young people questioned, seven were arrested and flown out to appear in court on assorted charges of illegal entry, possession of marijuana and cultivation of same, possession of firearms. All seven were subsequently deported from Canada.

This was a tremendously exciting happening, and the community was a busy, gossipy place for a few days. We even made front page headlines in one of the northern newspapers: "DRUG RAID IN NORTH!" The raid had been instigated by immigration officers, but the vice squad came along, too. Evidently the kids had been too vociferous about having crossed the border illegally, about intending to live permanently in Canada, and about growing their illegal "grass" plants.

163

As in everything else there were exceptions in our general opinion of the hippies. Every so often one or two kids would arrive on the scene who seemed to be in search of something of value in their life style. They might be sporting long hair, beads and sandals, but there was also sincerity and a genuine interest in the area. We could spot this with no trouble at all, and even rented cabins at very reduced winter rates to some we really liked. There was John, the master woodworker, who paneled the walls of our kitchen-living room and built shelves and cupboards for us in exchange for a winter grocery order; there was another John who cut the entire wood supply for us and for all the cabins, also for his winter food supply; there were Bill and Liz, the beautiful couple, from whom we learned much about natural foods, improved cooking habits, first aid, and just generally living life to the fullest; there was Dick and Dennis, the friendly "terrible twosome", the "Mutt and Jeff" of the north country, who for a while together and separately brought the life of the party to whatever group of people they found themselves surrounded by at any particular moment, and who also introduced large-scale home-brewing onto the scene; there was Wally who was gathering information on bush living in order to perhaps teach a class at one of the "free universities" or write a book. (A proposed book outline had been sent to one of the major publishing companies, and an enthusiastic "go ahead" had been received in reply. Sadly, the book never did materialize.)

There was Jim, the frustrated young man with ulcers who wanted so desperately to get out of the city rat-race he was in and become self-supporting up north as we were doing. For three years he spent his summer holidays at Manson Lakes trying to make enough at gold mining to justify quitting a good paying job back in Vancouver. He was unsuccessful in these efforts, but while he was around we enjoyed him thoroughly. He had a unique, witty sense of humour, and in addition he was one of the best guitar players around. The second summer he brought another fellow to help him with his mining efforts and to introduce to our family when he came to town to visit with the Owens. Dave was a professional nightclub singer, so when he and Jim sat around our kitchen table in the evening, most of the conversation and fun was accompanied by guitar strumming, with Dave humming along or breaking into song every so often. It was delightful.

And then there was Dick Petersen, the middle-aged wanderer who came to us in search of a place where he could spend the winter while he looked around for a location to build his own home in the North. We liked Dick the moment we met him, and from his appearance and manner it was obvious that life was no financial burden for him. We spent half a day getting better acquainted with Dick and assured him of the use of one of our rental cabins for the coming winter. Since it was only mid-summer and we needed the cabins for a while longer, Dick said he'd take a run up to Alaska for a few weeks, but he'd be back.

He came back, and he was still the same shy, mannerly, unassuming fellow we remembered, but he'd had an experience to end all experiences. He'd tangled with a grizzly bear and lived to tell the story!

Somewhere along the Alaskan highway he had stopped the car and wandered over into the bush, presumably for a nature call, although the shy, ever-blushing Dick didn't say so. Suddenly he found himself face to face with the bear who was feasting on a moose-kill. Dick froze in his tracks, but the bear didn't. It charged and knocked him to the ground, swiping at him with huge paws. It didn't take much for Dick to "play dead" since that's exactly what he thought he'd be before long anyway. But the bear gave up soon and went back to his moose feast, returning only once more to slap Dick around a bit.

The bear eventually lumbered off, and when our hero dared to, he cautiously got up and made his way back to the car. The Alaskan Highway isn't a busy thoroughfare, so he had to wait in agony about twenty minutes before the first car came along and rendered assistance.

Dick spent several weeks hospitalized, recovering from the deep scratches and lacerations to his legs, arms, face, head and abdomen. He had merited a writeup in newspapers as far away as San Francisco, but that was the part that Dick, in his retiring way, didn't want. He even blushed apologetically while telling us this ghastly tale.

Dick stayed with us for two years and I always called him the most ideal tenant we ever had. He kept his cabin neat and tidy, and had plenty to occupy his time without the necessity of everyday visits and socializing. He seemed a rather brilliant scholar-type so whenever we engaged in evening roundtable discussions we'd take the philosophical approach to education, religion, state of the nation, daily living, and just anything which could be broken down into philosophical components. I often got lost along the way, but it was fun and stimulating. Larry affectionately called him a professional scholar, while I was of the opinion that he was engaged in some great writing program. Perhaps he was doing under-cover work for the U.S. Government, or perhaps writing a book or gathering material for a magazine. It all seemed unlikely, really, but it was fun to speculate upon.

While Dick was great with philosophy, literature, the typewriter, his card files and cross-index systems, still his attempts at practical living in the bush were somewhat amusing. He learned how to cut down a tree and chop it into firewood, and he learned all about wood stoves — the cooking on and heating with — but things mechanical were completely out of his realm. He had no hesitation in buying whatever was needed to work with and live more comfortably in the bush, and as long as directions came with the article — lamp, chainsaw, etc. — he'd figure he could make it work. Invariably, however, he'd get just so far and have to come over for help. After his first winter was accomplished and he wanted to get the battery back in his car, he asked where he could locate a mechanic to do the job. Evy could have accommodated him in this simple task, but to save face for Dick, Larry did it.

Somewhere along the way he heard about a good method of lining up future standing dry firewood by ringing trees. (One peels away a two-inch-wide band of bark from around the trunk of the tree. This prevents the sap from rising, and thereby kills the tree; but it remains standing until the time is convenient for cutting it down.) Dick thought this was an excellent idea, and since at that time he planned to stay in the area, and since he was a "do it now" man, he set about the ringing of fifty trees. This was acceptable except for the fact that about ten of them were bordering the road, and in an area just a short way out of town.

When he told us about this later, we both cringed noticeably. Dick being an observant and sensitive person, wondered what was wrong. We told him that the Forestry doesn't object to a reasonable cutting of trees for firewood by the residents, but they expect us to use discretion in choosing areas for cutting. Right beside the road didn't seem to be exactly the proper spot, especially since after the trees were cut there would be a big bare area instead of the natural woodsy landscaping.

Dick was mortified. He had been thinking only of his own convenience is getting the wood out, and now he was really worried because summer was just coming on, and the bared rings around the trunks of those trees were going to make them terribly obvious.

Attempting to lighten Dick's worries, and ever the humorist, Larry suggested he could paint the rings with dark brown paint to make the sin less noticeable — for the present, anyway. Dick laughed, but he must have gone home and thought about it because the next day he returned to ask if we had any brown paint! We couldn't believe he was serious, but he was. The next time we drove by the wounded area we had to look twice to discern the disguise.

Poor dear Dick. He wanted so much to be a northwoodsman, but the first fifty years of his life as a "white-collar man" were deeply ingrained. He returned to the States after a two-year effort. For a while we kept in touch, but have since lost all track of him. Whenever we speak of Dick, however, it's with compassion for his noble and worthy ambitions, and also with an accompanying lovable chuckle for his bumbling attempts. Actually I hope that contact with him will be established again. He was in a category all his own, and we did enjoy him.

For each of us, separately and together, these special years were the period of time during which we were meeting the few out of the many who were to influence our lives in a more than casual way. The girls met their future husbands during this period, and I sensed that I was losing mine. Had we been living at any of our former residences, this would have been a devastatingly lonely period for me with Larry so totally jade-involved; but at Manson Creek every day during "people time" of spring, summer and fall carried with it the possibilities for new experiences and new friends. For the average urban dweller living the average way of life, the circle of friends and neighbors is practically invariable and the pace of life predictable. Not so at Manson. Each time a car would drive into town I'd walk over to the store wondering what these particular people would be like. I often tried to put into words what it is about people which makes some of them immediately likeable: Is it the genuineness of a smile? The twinkle of an eye? An interested attitude? A cultured tone of voice?

There's never a problem describing people with a lousy attitude and unkempt appearance, and the sort of impression they create. But amongst all others there's something that makes a few stand head and shoulders over the masses, and I could spot this particular personality immediately. I suppose the extreme of outstanding first impressions could possibly be considered "love at first sight". I remember standing out front one day conversing with a senior government geologist who was waiting for a helicopter to arrive. We had just met and had been talking for only five minutes, but his British accent enthralled me, and I kept asking questions just to hear him talk. Before long his transportation arrived and he waved goodbye as they lifted off, leaving me with a silly, wonderful, exuberant feeling for the rest of the day. But there it was — the ultimate of good first impressions. What I'm really referring to, however, is the quick personality sum-up one makes when meeting strangers for the first time.

One day in early summer a young man appearing to be in his late twenties drove into town and stopped by the store. He was out of his new four-wheel-drive truck and walking toward me as I approached. Before he said a word I knew I'd like him. His black wavy hair was blown in unruly fashion and the corners of his eyes crinkled when he smiled. He was tall, thin, handsome, and talkative. Barry Parr introduced himself and we spent a leisurely hour chatting casually about the life here. He was up this way checking out an ad in a newspaper which concerned placer gold property near Wolverine Lake. Unlike others whom we'd laughed at for doing the same thing, this young man hadn't yet paid a cent. He was going to check out the property first. He had come from a responsible position as a chemist at the Atomic Testing

Site in Mercury, Nevada, and had left for his own philosophical reasons. He'd been carrying around a conflict concerning the project he was working on, and what he really thought about it way down deep. He was single and financially independent, so had decided to take a leave of absence and scratch around in the good solid earth for a while until some of his philosophical perplexities should untangle themselves.

We got Barry situated in a cabin and invited him over to share supper with us. The first impressions in this case were so good that I kept telling myself to go slow and not be too gullible.

A few days later when Barry had to make a trip back to Vancouver in connection with the property he was considering, he asked if there was anything he could do for us while he was out. Evy happened to be in need of a couple of tubes for his bike tires, and I hadn't yet figured where to send for them, so I handed Barry five dollars and a paper with the tube-size written down. As he drove off I made the statement that I felt I could have trusted him with five-hundred, and if my faith in my own impressions proved wrong, I'd willingly forego the money and charge it up to experience.

A week later Barry returned with not only the tubes, but with bags and boxes of beautiful fresh fruit for us — pineapples, papayas, peaches, bananas, and melons. I just knew I'd been right about him, but actually the whole family also shared my impressions.

Barry stayed at Manson for a couple of years and, while he was with us, became practically part of the family. Lyn and Les never had such a delightful big brother, or favorite uncle, or whatever role he seemed to fit. For a while the girls were waking him each morning by playing ball over his cabin, purposely making the ball bounce its way down the slope of the roof. Sometimes they'd open the front door just enough to let King go in and excitedly place his huge forepaws on the chest of the startled sleeping occupant, and lick his face. Barry took it all in the intended spirit of fun, and even seemed to enjoy the attention.

He couldn't tell us much about his former work because it was all shrouded in secrecy. At first a small part of my mind wondered a bit whether everything he was telling us about his life was actually true. Again, I shouldn't have doubted. A young couple who had worked with him in Nevada came up on their two-week summer holiday to see what their friend was up to. At the time they arrived Barry was away on a short trip to Germansen, so we invited his friends to come over for coffee to while away the waiting time. We discussed life in the States, life in Canada, and things generally, but when we asked about Barry, his friends left no room for doubt about the esteem in which he was held back at the Test Site. They said that whenever he wanted to return, his position would be there for him to take up where he'd left off.

Both the girls fell in love with him, each in turn, but Barry maintained the "favourite uncle" role. He was good for them, though, and was a good all-round family friend. It was he who provided the first financing for Larry and Stan when they needed helicopter money to bring Kellys One and Two to Manson from Ogden Mountain. He helped Lyn organize her jewelry-making talents into a business of her own. She possessed the skill, the tools, the workshop, the gemstone material, and the customers, but Barry helped her get it all together. He showed her how to take care of the small bookkeeping involved, and for her birthday he presented her with an assortment of stationery (paper, envelopes, invoices, etc.) all printed with an artistic letterhead which Lyn had previously designed. Although she had already enjoyed a measure of success in her project, Barry's interest provided her with the incentive and drive to work on building it into something which might, in the long run, turn into a lifetime vocation.

A few years later Barry was to become involved in the jade scene himself, forming his own mining company, working from a home base in Vancouver, and field bases in Ogden, Yukon, and other areas of northern Canada. However during the two years he was with us, Stan had also gotten himself settled in, and Larry was still around, so the winter months during these special years were something wonderful. The combination of brilliant minds, exceptional talents, and fun-loving personalities was unbelievable.

The living pace was always easy during winters. With short daylight hours and a late start every morning, all the routine chores would receive first attention — the woodcutting, any large or small building projects, water fetching, clothes washing, cooking, etc. But after suppertime the fun would begin. The back room of our home had been enlarged and re-designed with work tables all around the walls. The trim-saws and grinding and polishing equipment had been installed, and while this was primarily Lyn's workshop, still several people could work there without getting in each other's way. After Christmas one year, a new dart-board was affixed to the wall at the far end of the room. Thereafter the dart competition was fierce.

A few months before winter had set in, the fellows had constructed a large, two-storey A-frame building behind our house. This was accomplished under Stan's masterful direction and had been built as a warehouse and cutting room for jade. We christened it affectionately "The Jade Temple" and always referred to it as such even after it was no longer used for its original purpose. Although it was incomplete that first winter with only double plastic sheeting covering the window spaces, still a lot of jade-cutting was accomplished indoors. Stan had rebuilt a 45-gallon oil drum into a large, friendly wood stove. Lying on its side and set into a metal frame, this lovely heater could hold several three-foot split logs, providing warmth adequately for the downstairs room of the building. Another frame was welded together to fit over the top of the stove, for the support of a galvanized bathtub in which they'd melt snow into the necessary water for the cutting operation. Most every evening after the generator had been activated, the rock saw would be grinding away at a block of jade, while Larry and Stan, keeping a check on the water supply and the progress of the cut, would have their heads together over a chess board. They matched their wits over a game or two every evening.

The previous winter had been a quiet one with no outsiders around, so many evenings Larry and I had spent a couple of hours teaching our daughters to play the card game of Hearts. When they had mastered this, we advanced them to Bridge. Our evening routine that winter had been an hour or two of jewelry work, and then a couple hours with the Bridge lessons. So while the girls had become rather proficient card players, still none of us every over-emphasized that particular recreation. It took its proper place as an acceptable time-killer if there was nothing better to do.

Somehow, most of the time there seemed to be better things to do when Stan and Barry were with us. Many evenings we indulged in a game of our own devising, and had a lot of educational fun with it. Someone would pick a word from the dictionary which he thought would be unfamiliar. Going the route of animal-vegetable-mineral, or "twenty questions", the rest of us in turn around the table would attempt to guess the meaning of the word. Ever heard of mucid? Or nevus? Spelt? Sneck? Rip-rap? Lipide? Exiguity? Edacity? Crampon? Boscage? Tabescent? Schnorrer? The dictionary is full of good, usable words which the average person isn't even vaguely aware of. We had lots of fun with this game during many a cold winter evening.

Anyone's birthday, or Valentine's day, or any occasion at all could provide an incentive for baking a fancy cake or a monstrously big pie made in a twelve-inch frying pan, or some other goodies from the oven. The men around the area were more than eager participants in the consuming of anything homebaked, and their appreciation made it fun to do.

One particular Hallowe'en was nothing short of a terror campaign. Lyn and Les were determined that the day was going to be outstanding, and things got off to a good start by putting salt in the sugar bowl. Doug Jack from Germansen was the girls' first victim. He had stopped in to say hello and have a cup of coffee before traveling on down the road. We all appeared casual, as usual, as we joined him with coffee, but actually never was our concentration more acute, watching for that first reaction after he had stirred a couple of spoonfuls of salt into his delicious brew and tasted it. Words are inadequate at this point. It was beautiful! Doug never trusted us again. For all the times he had coffee with us thereafter, I don't believe he ever failed to comment on the experience and taste a bit of the sugar before putting it into his cup.

Several others went the same route before that particular trick grew stale. By evening everyone had shared ideas about the Hallowe'en tricks they'd witnessed or participated in, and the fracas was in progress. Out-house doors were nailed shut, and after they'd been forced open, some other gremlin would sneak in and dribble honey on the seat, or sprinkle sand, or both! Leslee personally smeared honey on almost every doorknob in town, but our delighted satisfaction was in watching her reaction when she went to open her own bedroom door and found a sticky mess in her hand. Retribution is most rewarding!

The girls furtively gave Barry's white cat a bath in some dark-brown hair rinse which I happened to have on hand. Truthfully, the only thing recognizable about the cat was its typical Siamese meow.

While Stan was busy elsewhere, the kids removed from his cabin all the light bulbs, candles, lamps and matches. When he went home there was absolutely nothing he could do but go to bed.

Car and truck windows were soaped, of course, and potatoes stuck into the exhaust pipe of several vehicles, rendering them impossible to keep running.

No one wanted Johnny to feel left out of things, so while a couple of fellows kept him occupied in a game of crib, the rest of the gang draped toilet paper back and forth silently over the roof of his cabin, and all over the surrounding trees and bushes. They wasted about four rolls of paper, but the effect was tremendous. It looked more like a shivaree than like Hallowe'en, but it was beautiful. Johnny's place was the center of attention for several days, until the streamers broke up and blew away, or were taken down.

During the daylight hours on Hallowe'en there had been new snow falling. About three inches of fluffy stuff covered everything in a smooth and beautiful white mantle. But looking out next morning, there was hardly a square foot of that smooth white mantle that hadn't been trampled. Must have been a lot of busy feet around town the night before!

*   *   *   *   *   *

The next people who walked into our lives during these special years, and created uniquely precious memories, were the Christian Schmidt family. We first met them when they drove in to Manson on a tour of the north country, in search of a homesite in Canada. Les had gone over to the store, and being immediately favorably impressed, had invited them over to the house for coffee.

As the smiling fortyish-appearing couple walked through the door followed by three teen-age sons, Mr. Schmidt stated, "Your charming daughter has most graciously invited us over to meet your family. We're truly honored. This is my wife, Janet, and our sons, Mark, Gray, and Dale."

Had this statement been the only words we ever heard from him, the effect couldn't have been lessened; but for the next couple of hours we sat entranced. Larry and Chris monopolized the conversation, but we were all happy to have it so. It was a question and answer session, and our new friends were eager to learn everything about our rural way of life. Their plan was to spend this summer holiday looking for the area they would enjoy, and then after having chosen a place to build, they'd go back home to Minnesota, sell their house, and spend the winter getting ready to make the big move to Canada the following summer.

The Schmidts' interests and involvements seemed to cover a wide spectrum — everything from ecology to symphony. They had been instrumental in accomplishing the cleanup of a polluted river back in Minnesota, and although it had taken the equivalent of volumes in letter-writing, and a great deal of time and hard work, the feeling of accomplishment after two years of effort had been worth it all. They were tree-planters, and had had hundreds of saplings either started, or thinned out from overcrowded areas and transplanted to where they could better survive.

Music was a big part of their lives. They had an enviable collection of classical records, and a quality sound reproduction system. Each member of the family had learned to play musical instruments, and the boys all had reached the intermediate stage of proficiency. Janet, a concert violinist, is still involved with the Minneaplis Civic Orchestra, with string quartets, and is frequently engaged for professional solo work.

Our jade discovery and Lyn's jewelry-making added a large dimension to their interest in our particular lifestyle. Chris himself was a jewelry designer-artist. As to the caliber of his work we were not fully aware until we'd come to know him much better.

The Schmidts camped in our area for the summer, travelling the fifty miles up and down the road, checking out all the branching byways, getting acquainted with all the residents, and always keeping a watchful eye out for some exactly right spot that would appeal to all of them as a homesite.

172

The weather was ideal, and all sorts of good things seemed to be happening in just the right timing to convince them that this was a wonderful country. They even had the rare opportunity of playing foster-family to a newborn moose for a few hours. One of the boys happened to be looking in the right direction at the right time and saw the baby moose scrambling up out of the creek onto higher ground, right in the middle of Schmidts' camp. Seeing human beings, probably for the first time, the little moose just stood there on its wobbly legs and shivered, either with cold, or fright, or both. Where was its mother? Anyone who knows anything about wildlife knows that the only thing more dangerous and deadly than a charging bull moose in rutting season, is a cow moose with her young offspring. The protective maternal instinct in the moose family is something to behold and respect.

Before long, word got around that there was a newcomer in town, and a small sized crowd had gathered to pay their respects and to speculate on just why this baby was alone. Not one of us felt complacent, however, about our immediate vulnerability, and we kept scanning the surroundings for an approaching irate mother moose. All we could figure was that since the little one had emerged from the creek, the mother and baby must have been separated by the rapid current while swimming from one side of the river to the other. Therefore, mama moose must be over there somewhere. But even with binoculars we scanned the opposite hill to no avail. In desperation we finally decided to walk the little one into the trees a couple hundred yards out of town and within sight of the creek. Surely the fantastic maternal instinct would bring mother and baby together again. Evidently it did. Next morning a search of the general area revealed no sign of either moose.

The Schmidt Family were enthusiastically happy, and we were the beneficiaries. The instant compatibility between our two families — which had done nothing but increase the more we grew to know each other — was rare and stimulating. We found Chris to be a brilliant conversationalist, a true perfectionist in his work and in every phase of his daily living, and altogether a truly wonderful person. Together with his lovely and talented Janet and their three boys, each individualistic in his own right, this was a family the likes of which I have never encountered. My personal satisfaction in conversations with Chris has been in the realm of discussion periods. He's a blend of both teacher and learner — both interesting and interested. While talking is obviously his forte, he is also an equally proficient listener. I've found it impossible to have a frittering, worthless conversation with him — ever. Around many a campfire we have all sat exchanging thoughts and ideas, sometimes even until the first hint of dawn in the east.

Before they left to return home to Minnesota, Chris added the finishing touch to a spontaneous and growing friendship by presenting to us a beautiful book entitled *Encounter With Art*, co-authored by himself and an artist friend, Reid Hastie. It had been recently published and was intended as a college textbook for the study of art and art appreciation. It was lavishly illustrated. Chris autographed it for us and we consider it a family treasure.

Letters went back and forth all winter. Chris and Jan kept us informed of the progress of their intended move. Selling their home was no problem since it was a picture-book type dwelling, built into a hillside and ruggedly individualistic. In fact, it had been photographed and featured in one of the Minneapolis *Tribune's* Sunday Magazines.

The one major setback which no one could have anticipated was the discovery of a malignant growth in one of Chris' facial glands. The vital, necessary surgery left him unaccountably weak so the big move to Canada had to be postponed. The whole thing was a blow to them and to us. The Schmidt family, however, invited Lyn to stay with them for a while so she could advance her jewelry designing career under the direct tutelage of Chris who had observed her ability.

This marvelous opportunity happened at exactly the right time for Lyn. Every summer she had been enjoying a brisk business with her jade jewelry, but still something was lacking. With all the travelers through Manson observing the outdoor rock-saw cutting operation, naturally many of them wanted to buy a piece of raw jade or some finished jewelry or both. Especially thrilling were the times when a helicopter would circle town, set down in the yard, and the emerging passengers would inquire for the jade artist they'd heard about. These visitors would often be executives of mining companies with exploration teams working in the North. They were interested in seeing the processing of jade boulder, and would invariably buy a piece of the raw material and/or some finished jewelry to take back home with them. Lyn was providing them with earrings, broaches, pendants, rings, and bracelets, with prices varying from eight dollars to fifty, depending on quality and cost of the findings (backings) and the amount of her time involved in styling and shaping the particular item.

This much attention and activity would have been enough to keep a mere "piece-worker" happy, but it wasn't satisfying the "artist" in Lyn. The routine of cutting and polishing a piece of green stone to fit into a machine-made ring-mount was becoming stifling. She was missing the creative part of the job. Already she was weary of being a mere technician, and felt that there was something more for her somewhere. In perfect timing the Schmidt Family's generous offer came along and

Lyn headed for Minnesota to work and learn alongside Chris for a few months.

While he was humble where his talents were concerned, we had learned that Chris was one of twelve designer-craftsmen in the United States whose jewelry creations had been selected for exhibition in the Brussels World's Fair in 1958. His work has been on display in galleries and museums throughout the States, and Chris has instructed Art and Design in both public schools and art institutes for many years. But what really impressed us the most was discovering his name and pictures of some of his work illustrating certain processes in silversmithing in other textbooks on the subject. We were thrilled that a man of this stature would recognize and be interested in helping to foster Lyn's artistic ability. It was an invaluable opportunity and she absorbed the learning well, as evidenced by Chris's letter to us later:

". . . She has handled a variety of metal-working techniques very well, and her design sense is excellent. She is the best student I have ever had who combines excellence in both design and technique. She is so receptive and hard-working that she will go just as far in jewelry-design as she wants to . . ."

But it wasn't only in the workshop where she was learning. Besides absorbing all the processes involved in transforming a piece of flat silver sheet into an intricately beautiful object of art, Lynlee was also being treated to a course in "family life." Here was where she observed a dedicated husband and father in action and began realizing what she had been missing at home. Chris was so interested in everything of value which can influence a life that he made curiosity and observing and learning fun for everyone associated with him. "Family togetherness" most appropriately describes the attitudes of the Schmidts. Unlike most urbanites, Jan and Chris were dedicated and devoted to the providing of unending learning experiences for their boys; and for the time Lyn was in Minnesota, she became the daughter they'd never had, and was treated to all the fun and learning, too.

They wrote often telling us what a lovely girl we had, how nicely she was fitting into the family scene, and how much they enjoyed having her there. Lyn also wrote often telling us of all the new experiences, trips and visits to places of interest and of all the unusual people she was meeting. Chris and Jan's intimate friends were mostly artists and intellectuals, but on a day-to-day basis Chris had such a unique way of bringing out the worth of the individual — just in his intense interest and concern with people — that he often hob-nobbed with the proprietor of the corner barber shop.

The place where the Schmidts were living was a small town outside of the Minneapolis metropolis. The town was duly proud of its celebrity and kept an eye on his activities. Before Lyn left to come home the local newspaper ran a picture of her at work, with Chris standing by, and an accompanying article, part of which read:

"A twenty-year-old Canadian woman returned to her home after having studied contemporary jewelry design for ten weeks with Jordan's renowned artist, Christian Schmidt . . ."

*   *   *   *   *   *

Christmas seasons every year were special to me since I'm basically the sentimental type; but the holiday times during those special "best years" were memorable in unusual ways. The December 10th we received word that Larry's father had died very suddenly, a shadow was cast over our festive mood. Immediate plans were worked out for Larry to fly down to California to be with Mom in the difficult days ahead. I had wanted to go but we didn't feel we could leave the kids alone in the middle of winter, so I elected to send Lyn along to represent me. Les and Evy and I were left once again to handle the place by ourselves, but this time we weren't alone. This was happening during Stan's first winter at Manson and he was tremendously helpful as the man-around-the-place in Larry's absence.

That had been our first Christmas as a broken family unit, which alone could have made it memorable; but Stan provided the festive touch. Each evening during Christmas week we asked him in to dinner by candlelight — the better to appreciate the colorful lighting from the beautifully decorated tree. Afterwards we lounged around "comfortable" for an hour or two listening to selected music from the record player which Stan had generously donated to our household, along with several boxes of assorted albums of music. That had been a most peaceful Christmas.

A year or two later, after Lyn had had her training in jewelry design, she presented to me a Christmas gift of a silver and jade ring which she had created in its entirety. Many hours of planning and work had gone into that gift, and while she was modestly pleased with the effort, I was proud and delighted.

One of the more recent Christmasses Stan hung a note on the tree, addressed to me, and stating that during the following week he would install the fluorescent light fixture in the ceiling of our kitchen-dining room. This may not appear to be anything so special until one understands that that fixture had sat in its carton for two years. We had bought it to replace the unsightly and inadequate light bulb which hung over the table. Larry had fully intended to install it, but it just never got to the top of his priority list. I had given up hope and actually had forgotten about it until Stan came through with that delightful gift of his time and labor. The difference in both appearance of the room and effectiveness of the light was sensational.

The Schmidt family did eventually move to Manson and accepted our offer of the use of a couple of cabins until they could find their own building site. Their first Christmas here was a new experience for us. We were invited over for an after-dinner drink and some record listening-to in their "studio". The new cabin (which they had masterfully built in record time) had been christened "The Studio" because that's exactly what it was — an arts and crafts workshop for the family, and a place of learning for anyone interested. Inside had been set up the thousands of dollars worth of tools, equipment and materials which represented a lifetime occupation in jewelry design and creation. But also inside the Studio was installed their stereo system.

This Christmas night Chris had selected for our listening pleasure the opera "La Bohème", and after he gave us a verbal resume of the plot and libretto, we sat back entranced for the next few hours.

Another Christmas brought the first announcement of impending matrimony. Although Leslee was only seventeen then, and Stan considerably older, they made a striking twosome and were delightful together. Tall, attractive and exuberant, Leslee possessed the ability to act in a mature, dignified manner if the situation required it. Basically she was a light-hearted creature of the wilds, often taking walks along the creek or through the bush, and always finding something of interest to bring back — an unusually beautiful rock, an intriguing piece of driftwood, an ancient and completely white mooserack, or a skull of small small animal long since dead.

Although Leslee's favourite sport seemed to be playing the role of delightful nuisance, she also had depth. She could lose herself completely in a good book for hours on end. As with Lyn, Les had reached the level where the work load of Correspondence School lessons was becoming unreasonably burdensome, and the dilemma had arisen as to how to achieve the Grade Twelve diploma. Eventually she had come up with the idea of making the trip back to California to live with Larry's mother and to go to public school there for a year. Grandpa having died the previous year, Leslee's presence might also provide some company for her grandmother. The prospect was a happy one for all concerned.

The adventure wasn't completely satisfactory, however. Before the year was over, Les was finding that she couldn't take it any longer. Her work was excellent, but she was too homesick for the north woods, for the family, and for Stan. She was never suited to city living — at least not after having experienced the peace and solitude of the wild country for so much of her life.

After making it very clear to us and to Stan that she was never going to settle for being "just a housewife" (which really meant that she wanted to marry Stan, but she also wanted to fulfill herself as a person), Les began working out wedding plans with us.

Granting our blessing to this union was not difficult, somehow. Stan had endeared himself to us all in the few years he'd been around. He was talented in diverse fields, from mechanics to music appreciation. He was strong, yet gentle; intense at times, and a life-of-the-party type at others. He and Larry as prospecting partners had worked well together and had compromised intelligently on any differences they might have had from time to time. Now as business partners in the promising jade enterprise, Stan's financial future seemed as secure as our own — perhaps more so, since it seemed to me that Larry's and my share was going to be split again when we went our separate ways, while Stan's would remain intact in a happy marital situation.

The wedding took place in Vancouver where Stan and Larry at the time were deeply involved in the organizational aspects of their business there. We all flew out from Manson to Vancouver where we met, for the first time, Stan's parents and relatives who had arrived from Alberta. The ceremony was a lovely fireside affair with a catered buffet supper afterward.

The newlyweds set up temporary housekeeping in a modern sixteenth-floor ocean-view apartment and were happy there for a while, but after a few months both were yearning for the north country. Something had to be done. It was not long until Stan and Larry sat down to talk out the future involvement for each of them in this jade business. Larry was finding it all stimulating and challenging right where he was in Vancouver, and Stan was more than happy to move back to Manson and accept the responsibility of taking complete charge of the operation at the mine site every summer.

That was a perfect arrangement for the men, but Larry's position as head-of-household became, in effect, completely vacated. It was no surprise, however. I sensed that it was coming, and the rest of us had become so accustomed to running Manson Creek in Larry's frequent absences that it didn't seem to make a great difference. Even before the jade-find, he had lost interest in rebuilding and improving things around the townsite, and it was this department where a man was sorely needed. But as for the vacancy in the father role, the girls were grown up by this time, and Ev had grown accustomed to not having his father around.

I deplored Larry's lack of family involvement, however. When he was so-inclined he had so very much to give that I worried a bit for Evy's not being able to draw from his Dad whatever and whenever he needed.

Since our youngest continued to be involved in just about everything going on at Manson, and since he had so many "big brothers" to do things with, I don't really believe he had a sense of missing anything or anyone. Perhaps some consequence of this lack may show up later, but Evy was such a busy little boy with so many, many people, he couldn't have felt lonely very often.

When Stan and Les drove back into Manson, after being away a few months, Stan jumped out of the car and in an over-dramatic gesture kissed the good earth and opened his arms to all the beautiful green surroundings. Les was equally joyous. Those two will never live full-time in a city, I'd guess with positive assurance.

The kids gave some thought to buying and taking over Manson. There was a world of work-possibilities for someone like Stan who was adept at building, remodelling and improving. They seriously considered it, but neither one was willing to be at the beck and call of the public at the store and gas pump, and there'd never be sufficient revenue to warrant hiring someone to take over that part of the operation. They decided just to live in their little cabin across the creek. Les continued with her schoolwork by correspondence, and for a couple of summers worked with Stan and the crew on Ogden Mountain.

Yes, those were the good years.

A Northern Wedding 33

While those may have been the outstanding years of our decade at Manson, they were certainly not the end of unusual and memorable happenings. If we stayed another ten years the incidents would go on and on. With this "expect the unexpected" way of living, there were occasional stretches of time when life seemed to be at a standstill, but invariably, before long someone new appeared or something different happened to click the shutter and open our thoughts to another situation.

It was apparent that Lyn was becoming a bit restive. She was an adult, doing a lot of thinking for herself, deploring the lack of cultural and artistic stimulation at Manson. I could sense that she wasn't going to stay here indefinitely. No plans had been forthcoming from her as yet, but whatever was stirring in her thoughts was postponed for a while with the arrival on the scene of Bill Joiner.

Bill was a young man who, after graduation, had spent a few years "exploring" Europe with friends. He had been born in the Yukon Territory, but grew up in Vancouver where his father was, and still is, a practising Doctor of Dentistry. Upon returning home from Europe, Bill chanced to hear about the jade workings and went over to the Vancouver plant to inquire about a job. He was hired and turned out to be a receptive, eager learner. It wasn't long before Bill had become a reliable man around the shop and effectively conversant on the subject of the material he was handling.

It was inevitable that Bill was to hear a great deal about both Ogden Mountain and Manson Creek, and after spending an evening with Les and Stan on one of their Vancouver trips, he decided he was just going to have to see this north country, live there a while, and maybe even get a chance to work on the mountain at the source of this exciting jade product.

180

Subsequently, Bill made his way to Manson and took up residence in one of our cabins. We invited him to dinner a few nights until he had grown used to the "roughing it" routine. Then he was on his own. It had never been our custom to make it easy for any of the young people who thought they wanted to live up here. We actually encouraged, and almost forced, complete independence in all the newcomers, our theory being that if the kids wanted to get away from home and family, then nothing is gained in experience by practically moving in with another family somewhere else.

Bill settled in easily and naturally, cooperating with the work and play efforts around town. He was intrigued with Lyn's branch of the jade business and wanted to learn what she could teach him about the art of polishing cabochons and setting them into jewelry. Being an eager learner, his proficiency increased to the extent that eventually Lyn let him take over at the jade workbench. She always kept a supervisory eye on his work, and no order was ever filled without her strict, critical approval. This arrangement left Lyn free to begin working with the silversmithing equipment she had been accumulating since her recent apprenticeship in Minnesota.

A year later when Lyn and Bill decided to become "Mr. and Mrs.", which actually was no surprise, we had a new and exciting prospect to plan for — a wedding! It would be the first in Manson Creek that anyone could remember. We decided on an outdoor ceremony in keeping with the natural simplicity of the surroundings, and a barbecue-picnic afterward. Informal invitations would go out to all our friends up and down the north road.

From the time of decision to the date of the ceremony there were only two months to complete all the preparations — the most complicated being what to wear. Lyn decided on a pant-suit, which in turn created a major problem. She was a size-nine type but very amply "blessed". If the jacket were the right size, the pants would be two sizes too large. Similarly, if the pants were to fit, the jacket would be two sizes too small. Bill came to the rescue, suggesting that his mother knew a professional dressmaker in Vancouver who might be able to solve the problem if we could work out the details and send the information down to her.

Well now, this was a challenge of my proficiency in the mail-order department. First step was to draw a sketch of Lyn and write in every possible measurement that might be required. We cut out a catalogue picture of approximately what she wanted, drawing in only a few changes in collar and neckline. A detailed description of color and texture of desired fabric was included. All this information was mailed to Bill's mother and sister who, in turn, consulted with the couturiere and then went shopping for the material. The whole order was plunked in the hands of the seamstress. We all suffered a few trepidations as the day of the wedding drew near, because we weren't going to be able to see the bride's ensemble until the Vancouver contingent of the family would be arriving with the package. This was cutting things uncomfortably fine.

Larry came for the wedding, traveling with Bill's parents and family. They jetted to Prince George and then transferred to a bush plane for the remainder of the trip. Arrangements had been made with Archdeacon Yarborough of the Anglican Church in Vanderhoof to fly in for the day to perform the ceremony. With such a big part of the actual wedding being dependent on a few days of good flying conditions, I'm sure the Great Weather Man must have been swamped with petitions as the time drew near.

We needn't have worried for a moment about Lyn's outfit. When she put on the suit it was a perfect fit — everywhere — and she looked delightful. I think we were all amazed that something so complicated and detailed could be accomplished so satisfactorily at long distance. And from then on I considered myself a Master of Arts in "mail order".

The wedding day dawned bright and clear. It was a perfect warm June day, made to order for the occasion, and too early in the season for the annoyance of blackflies and mosquitoes — an important consideration in the north latitudes. The minister arrived on schedule and we all stood around on the grass, rather informally, as the rites were read.

A barbecue-buffet meal and cold drinks had been set up in a pavilion, so the whole afternoon local people from up and down the north road were dropping in, staying around a while to participate in the conviviality, and extend their good wishes to the newlyweds. Any of the regular delivery men driving the road that day were invited over for a drink and a lunch plate, as were also a few casual tourists. When a helicopter circled, landed, and its pilot came striding over to the area of activity, we all wondered what message he might be bringing. It was strictly a social call, however. He'd been on an assignment farther north, and having heard about the wedding and knowing most of us through work with the jade operation, he decided on the spur of the moment to take a run over to Manson to extend his personal good wishes. Lyn was thrilled, amazed and delighted at having this visitor drop in literally out of the blue.

The fun and socializing went on all day. In the evening a huge bonfire added its glow to the occasion and several of us sat up long into the night enjoying the warmth and friendly discussions which firelight always seems to engender. It had been a day to remember — a day to treasure in our vast and ever-growing storehouse of memories.

Mr. and Mrs. Joiner moved into one of our larger cabins and Lyn discovered, to her great satisfaction, that Bill was a more-than-willing "house husband". He loved to putter in the kitchen, concocting tasty dishes, and not even minding the cleanup afterwards. He had already mastered the art of woodstove cooking, and we were all benefiting from his efforts. At one time Bill had seriously considered studying in Europe to become a professional chef.

Les and Stan, together with Lyn and Bill, combined their efforts in a number of work projects, the outstanding one being a capacious twenty by thirty-foot summer greenhouse which Stan masterminded. Sixteen planting beds inside the heavy plastic, log-framed construction were producing remarkable crops the likes of which we had never seen grown at Manson. There were turnips, carrots, beets, onions, vegetable-marrow, radishes, lettuce, zucchini, spinach, and probably more. Soil for the project had been enriched with loads and loads of peatmoss, brought in by truck from a mile away where Stan had discovered a natural source. Water was a problem. A powerful, portable pump, capable of lifting water from the creek up the thirty-foot embankment, would fill several 45-gallon drums which had been set up inside the greenhouse. From these the plants were hand-watered several times a day. The thermometer had to be watched. On a warm summer day the temperature inside might register 130 degrees F., which was tremendous for the plants, but in only a few weeks, nighttime temperatures might suddenly drop to near freezing, necessitating a fire in the little air-tight heater which had been installed.

Those beautiful vegetables were indeed nurtured with a lot of tender loving care, and the difficulties involved might have discouraged any but the determied. But the Poraykos and Joiners were determined! In fact, that greenhouse became a small local tourist attraction for a couple of summers.

This congenial foursome were back and forth to each other's cabins often, sometimes for morning coffee, occasionally for dinner. They took walks or snowmobile trips together, played bridge most competitively many an evening, experimented with the brewing of beer and wine. The Jade Temple, which no longer was used for its original purpose, became the perfect setting for a standard-size ping pong table, allowing lots of room for maneuverability of the players. Together with the men from the Schmidt household, competition was fierce. Hot and heavy ping pong tournaments were in progress all winter that year.

Life was rich and full and fun.

A New Mineral Emblem

There's no question that Larry and Stan's jade discovery has been the greatest single event in our lives these ten years. There's been something in it for each of us. Lynlee has had her own special bit of popularity on the scene and is well on her way toward making a lifetime occupation in jewelry design and creation. Leslee married one of the successful prospectors and is reaping the benefits. Evy may someday be sharing this unusual story in a "show and tell" period in a public school classroom. For myself, I can't deny a certain pride in having been the wife of the "dreamer" who finally found a great something to make his life meaningful for him, even though the discovery and all its ramifications was the eventual untying of Larry's and my togetherness.

The discovery was also interesting to others, providing new learning experiences for those who had heard of jade but perhaps had never seen it or touched it. Our tourists, always full of questions, most frequently were amazed by the size of the "find" and wondered what on earth anyone could use all that jade for. After all, you can only make so may ringstones, and then what?

Well, although the Orientals have had a corner on the jade market for centuries, the Western world is now making its own claims. Most everyone loves jade and is proud to own a piece of it. Rockhounds hunt for it; lapidarians work it into jewelry; carvers shape it; wholesalers from all over the world order it by the ton. The newest development is in the construction industry. Flat, square-foot polished tiles (at $100.00 per tile!), made from less-than-gem quality material, are now being utilized as wall-facings and fireplace fronts in some of the new, sophisticated hotels, restaurants, office buildings, and homes. One twenty-ton boulder was taken intact from Ogden Mountain, sandblasted to remove the crust, and polished on one side. It was shipped to Osaka, Japan, to assume a place of honour in the 1969 World's Fair.

The Provincial Government, recognizing the previous jade finds in B.C., announced in early 1968 that jade was being adopted as the official provincial mineral emblem. At first we were happily astounded and felt a part of a history-making epoch, but later we realized that the decision had been made before Larry and Stan's discovery was known about, as evidenced by one sentence in the newspaper announcement: ". . . The only known source of jade in Canada is in the Lytton area of the Fraser Canyon . . ."

True, that area yielded B.C.'s only jade in any quantity for several years, but by the time our men were busy staking claims, the Fraser source was known to be running dry. So with the apparent quality and extensive quantity of the Ogden Mountain discovery, a better choice couldn't have been made for British Columbia's official mineral emblem. We had visions of blocks of jade and jade ornaments adorning the government buildings, offices, and desks. Possibilities were endless.

Only a few years before this, Richard Gump of San Francisco had written in his book, "Jade — Stone of Heaven" these words:

"Today there is no single source producing the uniformly fine-quality nephrite (jade) once found in Chinese Turkestan. The price of both raw and carved jade all too clearly reflects this fact. Each year as the supply decreases, the demand, and hence the price, increases . . .

"The world needs a jade mountain. Perhaps someday one will be found . . . Until then, and probably long after, fine jade will remain one of the earth's rarest and most coveted possessions."

Well, jade mountains will probably never be found, but our men's discovery of one of the most exciting jade deposits in the world will probably put the names of Stan Porayko and Larry Owen into the annals of B.C. mining history. That is no small achievement!

The "blessings" of the jade goddess hovered for a while longer. There were a few more intriguing happenings, such as one businessman (a prospective financial backer) going bankrupt as a result of the discovery of a shady deal he was trying to work — to his advantage, not ours.

I suppose, though, that even deities can be overwhelmed by the intricacies of our modern business world. Had it been possible for Larry and Stan to have financed the total operation themselves, the outcome might have been completely different. But not many average individuals can single-handedly raise funds to the tune of eighty thousand dollars for each three months of summer mining. And in addition to the mining there's also the marketing of the product.

Our men were most definitely "average individuals" financially. There was no way they could have found an "unattached" eighty thousand each summer. And as for the marketing, doing it unaided the fellows would probably have rented a warehouse in Vancouver and hired a few men to operate the saws. Their largest item of "overhead", after paycheques, would probably have been the telephone bills for long-distance calls around the world — a necessary expenditure in making contacts for bulk sales of the rock.

Unfortunately, it *was* necessary for them to obtain financial support, and in so doing they eventually lost control. (This is a common, sad truism in the world of prospectors.) Businessmen with money and a saleable product at their disposal do things far differently from our "small town" way of operating. After initially obtaining the warehouse, then came the offices, the secretary, the company cars, the salesman on the road, the "executive" salaries for the executives, the trips — first-class all the way — to Germany, China, Japan, and the practically unlimited expense accounts for lavishly entertaining prospective buyers. The money was going out faster and in bigger chunks than it was coming in. The hand-writing on the wall was apparent, and Stan and Larry sold out completely while they could still come out ahead. Stan worked for a while as consultant at the minesite, and Larry retained an office in the jade plant for a while, working as advisor in the cutting and shipping of the product.

Looking back, both men agree that regardless of how it all turned out, nothing could ever dim the thrill of the feelings they shared at the moment of their great discovery. That is their own special memory, and actually the high point of the whole jade adventure for them.

The men have plans for further prospecting, perhaps in the Yukon next time. Stan is a prospector at heart, and each summer Larry is ready and eager to take some time away from his thriving new gemstone business to get out into the field. They work well together.

A Glance over the Shoulder 35

Ever since we've been in the North I've frequently meditated over the fact that if the course of the Owen Family had been directed solely by me, we would have been just another of the nice, comfortable families in a nice, respectable, suburban neighborhood along with all the other nice, average people. Fortunately, this was not to be our destiny. Life with Larry has been anything but "nice and comfortable", but I have realized that all through the years I'd been trying my best to make it just exactly that.

Failing in any subtle efforts to re-design my husband, however, all I could do was go along with his far-out ideas — or leave him.

To think that in my more mundane attitude to life I might conceivably have missed out on this adventure if I'd planted my feet and refused, finally, to chase any more dreams! Larry was indeed a dreamer, and the world doesn't have much patience with this type of thinking in a person. It seems to be acceptable for a man to sit in his favourite armchair and roam the far corners of the earth, mentally, provided he recognizes this escape for what it is, and returns to reality after a brief indulgence in his fantasy. And every man is surely entitled to his annual two-week trek to mountains or seaside for the unwinding of work-frazzled nerves; but this must be accomplished in the allotted brief time so that he can return promptly to the necessary and vital task of earning the daily bread for the next fifty weeks. Work is necessary; dreams are impractical. Everyone knows this.

But just a moment now. Let me put the case for the Larrys of the world. Are dreams so impractical? With the authority of experience behind me, I'm prepared to say that while I might not have agreed wholeheartedly with this philosophy before, I'm now a convert. Although I haven't always applied it, I still maintain the truth of a bit of philosophy, peculiarly alive on the frontier, that insists that *anything —*

within the bounds of reason and physical possibility — anything one truly wants to do, one will find the time and the means to accomplish. But one must really be prepared to pay the price of achievement.

Most of the great human accomplishments in this world have resulted from someone of individuality, perhaps even painfully different from the run of men, stepping out of the well-trodden paths and "marching to the beat of a different drummer."

I don't know if meaningful conclusions for others can be drawn from our story. Nor do I know how appealing others would find a place as remote as Manson Creek for their brand of adventurous living. This little town has no special qualities that alone can give it unique balm for city souls. Many might hate its isolation. We just happened to land here, and while the area almost inadvertently provided Larry with his golden opportunity, it supplied a happiness and contentment for the rest of us to which the jade discovery bore only an incidental relationship.

I, personally, wouldn't have enjoyed the experience nearly so much without the stimulation of the tourists and the necessary duty-requirements of the store and post office. Yet others live up here in their log homes, satisfied with the good life, the generous helping of fresh air and blue skies, enjoying the complete diversity of summer and winter routines, unhurried schedules, productive existences, and contentment within their households.

It is indeed a good life here, but "good" is a relative term and must be interpreted by each individual for himself. For me it meant "tremendous!" For Larry, a few years would have sufficed. I can't really speak for my daughters since they've long since matured to the point of having ideas which don't always coincide with mine. We've had many discussions about the pros and cons of remote living, and while they may reserve a few more "cons" than I will agree with, still the fact that they are staying on with their husbands and making their homes here is evidence enough.

From the point of view of a parent, I'm convinced that these ten years have been far more than just the best we could have done for Evy and the girls. Every child, without exception, could benefit from a few years of rural living. There's something akin to character-building in the sharing of the work involved in making the family home function. Wood-cutting, water-hauling, ground-clearing, gardening, snow-shoveling, even stove-pipe-cleaning are all meaningful chores when they contribute to the total living pattern. What contribution can a city-bound child make to his completely automated home? There are mental gymnastics involved in solving a problem by using one's wits and coming up with a home-made remedy, rather than by rushing out to the nearest shopping center to buy what will solve the problem faster. Even such a simple thing as the fragrant aroma of frequent, necessary home baking goes a lot farther in welding family bonds, than any amount of packaged supermarket goodies could ever inspire.

Actually, I suppose it would be as difficult to start listing the advantages which these past ten years have provided to my family, as it would be to sit down and attempt to enumerate all the things one might have learned in four years of a college education. The real benefits are deep and are concerned with total attitudes and with people-to-people relationships. They are made up of intangibles, but they are there and will be influential in larger and smaller ways for each of us for the rest of our lives.

*　　*　　*　　*　　*　　*

With both of the girls happily married and living close by, I should have been completely happy and contented; but feelings of personal loneliness were gradually creeping into my consciousness. Larry had by now settled permanently in Vancouver, and his absence left a big gap in my life. When one is alone, life lacks a particular lustre. Regardless of how busy and happy I could appear to the public, to friends, and to family during the day, still the nights were becoming longer and lonelier. The prospect of another winter alone was disturbing — traitorous thoughts, but true. Could I find contentment elsewhere?

Coming to a definite conclusion about severing the ties and leaving our home of ten years was the eventual result of a good deal of soul-searching. The hesitancy wasn't from any fear of venturing alone into the world outside; rather it was a matter of how could I bear to give up the unique experiences involved with being proprietor of this little town, plus the incomparable associations with my daughters and their husbands and with all our special friends here.

What actually tipped the balance in this direction was my growing awareness of the need to get Evy into a regular classroom situation for his schooling. The Correspondence lessons hadn't been working for him any more than they had for the girls, but for different reasons. Lyn and Les, having had a good foundation in the basic "three R's" in public school, had found it relatively easy to pick up the new work and at least understand what was to be done without constant help.

But for Ev who started at Grade One in this unique method of schooling, it was vital for me, or someone, to be with him during the learning of so much of what he must learn. Let any distraction occur and "school was out!" for Evy. I'll never know how we got him through the first four grades. With all my store and post office duties, household requirements, and general tourist-type demands on my time, there just weren't enough hours in the day to do an adequate job of lesson supervision. I often thought about the time back in California when I adamantly declared I was *not* going to be the kids' school teacher during this northern adventure for which we were readying. Larry assured me that of course I wouldn't have to. He, a teacher and principal by profession, would be right there, wouldn't he . . . ?

*   *   *   *   *   *

So, the end of summer has arrived. The decision has been made, and Evy and I are packed and ready to leave for Fort St. James, a hundred miles south. A great deal of both literal and proverbial water has flowed under the bridge in this little town of Manson Creek, and in the lives of the Owen family. My daughters are enthusiastic for me, wondering how I could have enjoyed my aloneness for so long, and hoping that good things will happen when I get back into circulation again.

Arrangements have been worked out with Chris and Jan Schmidt's middle son, Gray, for taking over the ownership and operation of the town and store, so I'm confident that the place is being left in good hands. I have decided regrets about leaving, but certainly, as long as any of the family and close friends are living at Manson, we will return frequently for visits. We won't be that far away.

From the vantage point of Fort St. James we will be able to provide a sort of "halfway house" for any who might be traveling in to or out from Manson or Germansen, and who wish to stop in to visit and refresh themselves. This way I can keep a finger on the pulse of the area we love. And for Evy, the Fort boasts a lovely new and modern school which will be another whole new world for him.

Scenery-wise the place is almost an extension of Manson Creek, which was a contributing factor in my choice of towns in which to relocate. I'll never get lakes, trees, and mountains out of my blood now, and "the Fort" offers all these to my great satisfaction. The rest of the world can have the big cities; I think I'll never live in one again.

In the last mail there was a letter from one of the very special young men who spent some time up here. He had heard that we were leaving, and expressed his feelings in a way which said it all as well as or better than I could have:

"I'm sad to hear about the sale of Manson. Wish I could adequately put into words the deep and happy meaning in life which my time spent there provided. There was something at Manson Creek which I'm afraid I will not find again.

I wish I were as big as all outdoors and could wrap my arms around the area, the peace, the beauty, and the apparent happiness, and hang onto it, caress it, and protect it as a loving parent.

While this may sound strange coming from a man, it's the closest I can come to adequately describing the place and atmosphere I loved . . ."

And I say "Amen to that!", Jim.

Thanks to Larry's bent for adventure, and to the whim of fate which directed our topic of conversation with Bob and Carolyn around the fireside long ago, I found myself transported from a frantic pace of activity in busy Southern California to an entirely different scene in the sparsely populated North. Manson Creek grew on me, and in this particular setting, stripped of city nonessentials, I gradually learned and absorbed a great deal about rich, homely, in-depth life values.

The total scene at Manson was good for this Maggie Owen, and hopefully, Maggie Owen was in some measure good for this particular dot on the map — this "ghost town" which had been deserted by the gold miners of a century ago. Surely it is now a different ME from the one who first laid eyes on Manson. The influence of the type of life and living was my ally in holding my family together, in welcoming a host of people to adventurous holidays in the area, and in the enjoying and sharing of experiences with others who were footloose, undecided, and far from the places they called home, just as we had once been. If an atmosphere of warmth and friendship was possible for me to sustain and share with others, it was all a privilege I know now to be a rare experience, and to have been all in my favour.

I will not be going back to Los Angeles to live. It is somehow a proof of what Manson Creek has come to mean to me, that Fort St. James, on the southern shore of beautiful Stuart Lake, is as far south as I plan to make my home.